LEADING
IN EARLY
CHILDHOOD

SAGE was founded in 1965 by Sara Miller McCune to support the dissemination of usable knowledge by publishing innovative and high-quality research and teaching content. Today, we publish over 900 journals, including those of more than 400 learned societies, more than 800 new books per year, and a growing range of library products including archives, data, case studies, reports, and video. SAGE remains majority-owned by our founder, and after Sara's lifetime will become owned by a charitable trust that secures our continued independence.

Los Angeles | London | New Delhi | Singapore | Washington DC | Melbourne

GERALDINE DAVIS
AND GEMMA RYDER

LEADING
IN EARLY
CHILDHOOD

Los Angeles | London | New Delhi
Singapore | Washington DC | Melbourne

Los Angeles | London | New Delhi
Singapore | Washington DC | Melbourne

SAGE Publications Ltd
1 Oliver's Yard
55 City Road
London EC1Y 1SP

SAGE Publications Inc.
2455 Teller Road
Thousand Oaks, California 91320

SAGE Publications India Pvt Ltd
B 1/I 1 Mohan Cooperative Industrial Area
Mathura Road
New Delhi 110 044

SAGE Publications Asia-Pacific Pte Ltd
3 Church Street
#10-04 Samsung Hub
Singapore 049483

Editor: Jude Bowen
Assistant editor: George Knowles
Production editor: Nicola Marshall
Copyeditor: Audrey Scriven
Indexer: Silvia Benvenuto
Marketing manager: Dilhara Attygalle
Cover design: Wendy Scott
Typeset by: C&M Digitals (P) Ltd, Chennai, India
Printed and bound by CPI Group (UK) Ltd,
Croydon, CRO 4YY

Library of Congress Control Number: 2016931616

British Library Cataloguing in Publication data

A catalogue record for this book is available from
the British Library

ISBN 978-1-47392-947-0
ISBN 978-1-47392-948-7 (pbk)

At SAGE we take sustainability seriously. Most of our products are printed in the UK using FSC papers and boards.
When we print overseas we ensure sustainable papers are used as measured by the PREPS grading system.
We undertake an annual audit to monitor our sustainability.

CONTENTS

ABOUT THE AUTHORS

Geraldine Davis is a Principal Lecturer and Director of the Doctorate in Education at Anglia Ruskin University. She has worked in higher education for 14 years, following work as a teacher in schools, colleges and within the health sector, and led the Master's degree in Early Years Professional Practice between 2010 and 2015. She also headed a funded research project to explore the link between leadership in the early childhood workforce and outcomes for children from 2010–2013, co-edited the third edition of *An Introduction to Early Childhood* with Professor Tim Waller in 2014, and wrote the chapter 'Leadership and Change Management in Early Childhood'. With a passion for teaching and learning, alongside her research, Geraldine brings her considerable knowledge of professional learning, leadership in practice and child development to this book.

Gemma Ryder is a Lecturer in Early Childhood Studies at the University of East London. She started her career as a qualified Nursery Nurse and has worked in private and voluntary early childhood settings with the birth to five age group. She has worked closely with private and state schools and day nurseries as an Early Years Work Placement Coordinator at a college of further education and has acted as a trainer, assessor and mentor on the Early Years Professional Status (EYPS) and Early Years Initial Teacher Training programmes. Gemma is passionate about leadership and workforce development, which has been an integral part of her own research. Her connection to the early childhood sector and experience as a practitioner and lecturer bring a mix of practical experience and first-hand research to this book.

ACKNOWLEDGEMENTS

We are extremely grateful to the people and organisations who have given their time to contribute to the research we undertook for this book. Senior members of early childhood organisations have provided access to practitioners and details about organisational structures and ways of working which enhance their ability to improve outcomes for children. Their willingness to share their good practice with us has enabled readers of this book to benefit. We would also like to thank the universities and colleges who have supported us with our research and put us in touch with nannies, maternity nurses, parent consultants and childminders. Practitioners from a wide range of settings have willingly acted as participants in the research, sharing their experiences of leadership and enabling us to make this book 'live' for readers.

The authors would like to thank SAGE for their support and feedback as we developed this book.

INTRODUCTION

Leadership is a hot topic for early childhood and we advocate the use of leadership for all those who work in the field of early childhood education and care. The early childhood workforce has the potential to impact positively on the development of children and families. We have written this book to promote this potential through recognising the importance of leadership within the wide range of roles in the early childhood workforce. We use the terms 'practitioner' and 'professional' interchangeably in its chapters to identify the workers within the early childhood workforce. The book also makes use of examples of leadership from practice and will be useful for practitioners who are room leaders, team leaders and key persons, as well as leaders of settings, mentors, experienced or new practitioners. In the different chapters we promote leadership of early childhood practice across the range of roles that early childhood practitioners take, both within and across settings.

Typically, students of early childhood are practice focused. The most common obstacle faced in teaching students in early childhood is helping them overcome the lack of confidence they have in their abilities. This lack of confidence may show as lack of communication, lack of assertiveness, lack of control over one's own work, and lack of initiative. A further obstacle is their reluctance to link theory and practice, often through a belief that theory is too difficult and not for them. This book has practice at its heart. It examines specific early childhood practitioner roles and the everyday challenges and opportunities faced by practitioners in those roles. The activities and reflection points enable you to consider your role, and identify ways in which you can show leadership, and how you can then reflect on the leadership shown to take that leadership further. The text does not neglect theory, rather it draws theory into the practice-based discussions. Engaging with the activities will empower you through your development of greater confidence. The examples from practice also bring the book to life for you, relating to situations and roles you will be familiar with, to help you identify with the content. The practice examples also provide a useful link between the practice of leadership and theories of leadership.

Many different professional groups work with children, but not all of these professionals understand the different roles evident in early childhood practice, nor do they regularly attend meetings or engage with settings due to demanding workloads. This can lead to a lack of understanding of interprofessional practice. This book engages you with the interprofessional team and examples of working with that team to promote best practice.

Both authors developed an interest in leadership of professional practice through working with practitioners, and working with children and families. We have been able to discuss and consider opportunities for leadership within the different practitioner roles. We are of the view that leadership is for all practitioners, not just those with 'leader' in their job title. Both authors are academics, working in universities, but with the application of theory to practice driving that academic work. We are keen to promote the development of the early childhood workforce. Within this book, we have often focused on early childhood leadership practice in England, for example in the terminology used for different roles, and in reference to the curriculum. This is where our experience lies and from where our research findings have originated. However, we have drawn from the international literature and the book is relevant to early childhood practitioners internationally. We have also been careful to identify our sources so that practitioners are able to apply the principles of leadership within their setting regardless of the country they are working in.

We have undertaken original research in preparation for writing this book (Davis & Ryder, 2015) and are extremely grateful to the practitioners who have given their time to contribute to this research and the organisations which have provided access to practitioners and provided details about structures and ways of working. The research project is briefly summarised below and the findings from the project are separately being considered for journal publication. We deliberately sought the views of a wide range of practitioners (including students, early years educators, early years teachers, setting managers and setting leaders) across a range of settings (for example, voluntary, private, independent, small- and large-scale, home-based).

We have organised the chapters to support leadership in general as well as specific roles within the early childhood team. In this way the book can be read from cover to cover, or you can start at any of the chapters. Links to other chapters are identified within the text.

Within Chapter 1 we consider the scope of leadership of practice in early childhood settings and ask: who are the leaders, what do they do and what skills do they need? We then identify the range of leadership roles within early childhood settings, explaining the difference between leadership and management, and provide a summary of some theories of leadership, emphasising the importance of leadership across early childhood roles.

In the second chapter we engage you with two main ideas. Firstly, we discuss ideas that encompass practitioners leading children's learning. We identify the use of observation, planning and evaluation to support children's learning, and extend this to the use of reflection and assessment. Secondly, we consider the notion of leadership within the child, and ways to support the development of leadership within children as part of their resilience in life.

Chapters 3 and 4 consider specific early childhood roles, namely those of the room or team leader and the key person. We ask the question: what are the opportunities for leadership? We have included some scenarios and activities for practitioners who are employed in these roles. Within these chapters we also consider some specific qualities which an effective leader requires: assertiveness, resilience, communication and emotional intelligence.

Practitioners in early childhood settings are diverse. In Chapter 5 we explore leadership of this diverse workforce. We consider the diversity of staff and the importance of recognising different needs amongst staff. We also incorporate leadership of professional development within this chapter and consider opportunities and challenges in recruiting, employing and developing staff through the clarification of expectations, through planning, and through giving and receiving feedback and setting priorities.

Leading developments across a setting or settings is the focus for Chapter 6. We begin the chapter by discussing the importance of developing oneself, developing and empowering others, and developing a culture of leadership, so that settings do not rely on a single individual as leader, but instead distribute leadership roles within each setting. We then consider some of the structural factors which can support effective leadership and ways in which collaborative activity can occur within and across settings, sharing good practice. Also within this chapter we discuss the ways in which major changes can be introduced across settings.

Chapters 7 and 8 consider working relationships with people who are not employed by the setting, including families and members of the interprofessional team. Working with families to support the development of their children is seen as an important role for the practitioner. We encourage you to reflect on the accessibility of the setting to families, and the ways in which partnerships with families can be strengthened. We also identify the fact that some families need particular support, and the role of the practitioner in leadership in these situations. To extend understanding of the professional relationship, safeguarding of staff is considered. We consider aspects of working in a multi-skilled environment and how to be assertive and influence those from other professional groups.

The final chapter in the book is about using reflection to both celebrate and improve leadership practice. Reflective practice can help you consider your own values and beliefs and ways of working, and become more aware of how these affect the ways in which you lead people.

We hope you like the layout of the book. We have provided objectives for each of the chapters, scenarios from practice, and activities to support you in thinking about the material. At the end of each chapter we have also recommended additional reading.

SUMMARY OF THE ORIGINAL RESEARCH UNDERTAKEN (DAVIS & RYDER, 2015)

AIM

The overall aim of the project was to explore current experiences of leadership by people who work within early childhood practice settings. We were interested in the views of practitioners from a range of roles, some of whom were able to provide specific parental or family perspectives. Within this aim, the researchers aimed to:

→ identify the range of leadership practice which is taking place in early childhood settings;
→ celebrate effective practice;
→ identify opportunities to further develop leadership in early childhood practice;
→ make recommendations for leadership practice in early childhood.

RESEARCH QUESTION

In what ways do early childhood practitioners demonstrate leadership within their roles in early childhood settings?

PARTICIPANTS

Participants were early childhood practitioners within early childhood settings or parent consultants working with parents of young children. All 25 participants were aged 18 years or over and able to provide voluntary informed consent. The participants worked with children from newborn to age eight.

While we approached a range of settings, organisations and practitioners, only females participated in this project. We did not assess the number of men working in settings approached by us. The participants are summarised in Table I. 1.

Table I.1   Summary of participants

Qualification level
NVQ Level 2; NVQ Level 3; Foundation degree Level 4/5; Bachelor's degree Level 6; Master's degree Level 7.
Participants identified additional qualifications relevant to their roles. These included Early Years Professional Status; NVQ Level 4 management; Qualified Teacher Status.

Roles of practitioners
Level 2 practitioners; early years educators; senior early years educators; early years teachers; nursery teachers; Reception teachers; childminders; nannies; maternity nurse trainer; nursery teaching assistant; parent consultants; setting managers; room leaders; team leaders; key persons; play workers; support workers.

Geographic location of settings
UK – Essex, Suffolk, Norfolk, Nottinghamshire, Somerset, Devon, Greater London, Scotland
Channel Islands
Europe: France
Travel internationally on cruise ship or with families.

Types of setting
After school clubs; community playgroups; private nurseries; Steiner setting; Montessori setting; Forest School setting; Reggio Emilia setting; Reception class; independent school; nursery school; own home; family home, cruise ship.

METHODS

Sampling: Convenience sampling was used for the initial recruitment of participants. We approached settings, organisations and practitioners who were known to us through our work with settings and students, or recommended to us by practitioners, students, managers and placement co-ordinators. Initial contact was by email or face to face. Some snowballing of the sample occurred, through recruitment of further participants from the initial convenience sample. We sought to include a range of practitioners, a range of roles, and a range of settings. These were mainly, although not exclusively, from settings across the UK (see Table I. 1). Snowballing meant that some participants were located in Europe, or travelled with their role between the UK and other countries. The email invited participants to get in touch with researchers to express their willingness to take part in the project. If there was no response, no follow-up occurred. Those participants who responded were sent a participant information sheet and consent form and an interview or focus group meeting was arranged.

Research ethics: Best practice in ethical research was used following the ethical guidelines of the British Educational Research Association (BERA, 2011). Ethical approval was obtained from Anglia Ruskin University Faculty Research Ethics Panel.

Data collection: Data collection occurred through informal, semi-structured, audio-recorded interviews and focus groups. Interviews were held either face to face or by telephone. Face-to-face interviews were arranged at a mutually convenient time and place. Individual interviews were arranged where this was feasible, and focus groups were held when participants preferred to share their experiences in this way. All focus groups were face-to-face meetings. At the start of data collection we made explicit, both verbally and in the printed participant information sheet, that participation in the project was entirely voluntary and that participants would not be identified by name. Pseudonyms have been used to present extracts from the data. No personal details were collected.

Data analysis: Thematic analysis of the data enabled us to identify common themes across the data. Opportunities for and experiences of leadership within particular roles provided data to evidence leadership practice within the early childhood community.

RESULTS

The results of our research project are presented within the book, *Leading in Early Childhood* (SAGE, 2016), and are being prepared for presentation in early childhood journal articles and at academic and practitioner conferences.

SUMMARY OF FINDINGS

Early childhood practitioners work in diverse settings in the UK and abroad, and in diverse roles. These include sole responsibility for a child within a family or within a home setting; working in a consultancy role; responsibility for specific children within a room or setting; team leadership responsibilities; mentor roles;

developing novice and experienced practitioners; specific responsibility for emotional and social development of a child as their key person; leadership of practice within and across settings.

→ Opportunities to enact leadership are evident within a wide range of early childhood roles and settings. These include mentoring and supporting volunteers, agency staff and other practitioners; working as part of a team within the setting and with other types of early childhood providers; acting as agents of change; using new ideas and initiatives to improve and expand provision.

→ Confidence in knowledge and in role enables the practitioner to make use of leadership to positively influence early childhood practice on an internal and external level.

→ Values are important in early childhood settings, and are enacted through effective leadership. This includes leadership with children, families, other early childhood practitioners and other professionals. Valuing people includes respecting their autonomy and working to support inclusion and diversity.

→ Early childhood practitioners face a range of challenges and barriers to effective leadership. They meet these challenges by working collaboratively, liaising with other professionals and services, communicating effectively, setting clear goals, valuing the child, the family and the workforce, and recognising the importance of their role in supporting positive outcomes for children and their families.

→ Professional development is important for the early childhood workforce. This includes opportunities for formal and informal support with their specific role, opportunities for mentorship and networking, formal development opportunities, and engaging with research to improve and advance practice.

→ Early childhood practitioners develop emotional resilience to support their professional work with children and families. They use reflective practice to recognise existing effective practice, and to plan change to further develop practice. They work on safeguarding themselves as professionals and recognise issues pertaining to negative forms of practice.

→ Professional identity is clearly evident within the early childhood workforce. Early childhood professionals are important in positively supporting learning and development and educating children and families holistically. The importance of the role is not always recognised by families or by other professionals. Early childhood professionals acknowledge this and act as ambassadors for the early childhood workforce, detailing the nature of their roles and role-modelling effective professional practice.

1

LEARNING TO LEAD

CHAPTER OBJECTIVES

→ Discuss the meaning of leadership in the early childhood sector.
→ Consider leadership of early childhood practice and the knowledge, skills and confidence required.
→ Outline theories of leadership and their relevance to early childhood settings.

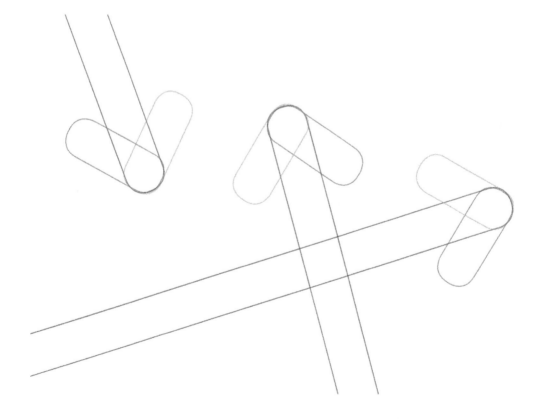

INTRODUCTION

What does the word 'leadership' conjure up for you? For many people the term is associated with individual job roles, with a job description which includes leading a team or an organisation. Thus, 'leadership' can be seen as the role of the 'big boss', the person who has the authority to hire and fire. In this chapter we aim to convince you otherwise, that leadership in early childhood settings is not the exclusive role of those who have 'leader' in their job title. We firmly believe that leadership can and should be part of everyone's role, and especially so in the early childhood sector. This chapter also sets out our values and beliefs about leadership, based on our own experience and the experience of early childhood practitioners from a range of settings. We hope that you will see the importance of these values, whatever your role in the sector.

WHAT IS 'LEADERSHIP' IN THE EARLY CHILDHOOD SECTOR?

In our view, leadership is about using your knowledge, skills, personality and experience to positively influence practice. Every practitioner has the capacity to lead, and by doing so to improve opportunities for children and their families and promote ways of working which support staff development.

We consider that some roles are identified as 'leader' roles, but that all early childhood roles need people who can enact leadership. Practitioners do this by enacting the values and supporting the goals of the setting.

ACTIVITY 1.1: LEADERSHIP AND MY ROLE

Think about the work you currently do in an early childhood setting: this may be a formal job role or an informal one, or it may be your role as a parent or relative. Thinking about this role, answer the following questions:

→ Do you know what the organisation or setting does?
→ Do you know what your role involves?

As an early childhood practitioner you have the potential for leadership in your role and you have the potential to positively influence practice. We suggest that you keep a notebook or journal as you work through the activities in this book. Make a note now about what the organisation or setting you work for does, and what your role involves.

The above activity is intended to demonstrate that every practitioner has some understanding of the setting for which they work, and at least some understanding of the role they have within this setting. Your role may be as an assistant, as the overall leader of the setting, as a SENCO, a teacher, a room leader, a key person, a nanny, or one of several other roles. You may have a job description, or you may have a number of tasks which are your responsibility. Whatever your role, you have a part to play. In this book leadership is seen as a component of every person's work in the early childhood sector. One participant in our research for this book, a senior early years educator, indicated what leadership meant to her:

> 'I think it means guiding and mentoring others, having the knowledge and confidence to deal with situations, and supporting others that have less knowledge of an area, so you can help them, and having ideas and implementing them and showing best practice, so others copy your good role model'.

Leadership may be taking overall responsibility for a whole setting or several settings, putting in place policies and procedures to enable the setting to achieve its aims, and providing a structure for the workforce to work with (therefore Chapters 5 and 6 will be particularly relevant to you if you are in this role). This is how many people view leadership, but leadership is much more than this. It might be looking for ways to do your own job more effectively, for example to work more productively with children and families, or to achieve the aims of the Early Years Foundation Stage. Chapter 7 considers ways in which all practitioners can promote positive ways of working with families. Leadership can include thinking creatively about your own work, how you might do something differently. Seeing leadership as part of your role can be empowering, it can make you feel you have an important role in the setting, and make others also realise the importance of their roles. Chapters 2, 3 and 4 aim to support such leadership practice within the practitioner role. Penn (2011) identified that there is a great deal that the early childhood practitioner *cannot* control about the setting in which they work, for example they cannot control the pay scales, or the curriculum, or government policy, or charges to parents. However, she also stressed that practitioners *can* control some elements of their work, and as such you do have control over the way you do your 'job on a daily basis' (Penn, 2011:149). As an example, one practitioner in our study, an early years educator, described that when she first started her job she suggested rearranging the way the room was laid out. As the room leader she discussed this with her manager and the other staff, and was encouraged to make this change. The very next day, furniture was moved around with the aim of improving the flow of the room: 'a home corner, and moving the cosy area away from the window, and moving the books … '. The other practitioners in the room were pleased with the way it made an improvement. This example demonstrates the leadership that practitioners can exert over their practice.

In early childhood settings leadership is different from what is the case in many other sectors. It is different because *context* is all important. Garvey and Lancaster (2010) point out that in the business world competency frameworks which measure leadership knowledge and practice are commonplace, but that they do not take account of the importance of experience and context in the enactment of leadership. For early childhood education and care, context is crucial and the experience of the practitioner within that context can build a strong culture of development. What is also important in the early childhood sector is that the characteristics of early childhood leaders are often distinct from those of leaders in other sectors, being 'kind, warm, friendly, nurturing and sympathetic' (Aubrey, 2011: 30). It is these same qualities which will support you to develop leadership in early childhood settings.

LEADERSHIP OF THE ORGANISATION AND LEADERSHIP OF PRACTICE

The different ways in which leadership is enacted are usefully identified by Whalley (2011b). In her consideration of the professionalisation of early childhood practice she identified two aspects of leadership, namely leading an organisation and leading practice. In this book we have devoted some chapters to specific roles within the early childhood workforce (leader of a setting, room leader, the key person). Here it is worth thinking about the overlap between leadership of the organisation and leadership of practice.

If asked the question 'What do leaders do?' three key elements spring to mind:

→   Leaders identify and enact values.
→   Leaders set the vision and goals.
→   Leaders ensure legal and moral responsibilities are met.

However, these aspects of leadership can be enacted at many different levels. For example, the identification of values for a setting will typically be led by the main identified leader within the setting (and Chapter 6 focuses on leadership across a setting or settings), but a collaborative leader will want to encourage all the members of a team to have their say in this. If you are a member of the workforce within a setting, you can show leadership through your willingness to contribute to the development and identification of these shared values. In his book which considers how organisations are structured, Morgan (2006: 137) discusses the 'enactment of a shared reality' and the value of this to the success of organisations. Early childhood settings have their own culture in which beliefs, vision and values are shared, and where children, families and community can be understood and supported through these shared values, vision and beliefs. Thus, the collaboration between various members of the workforce to undertake the job of leadership is important in the early childhood sector.

ACTIVITY 1.2: THE OPPORTUNITY TO LEAD

Thinking about the setting in which you work, or a setting with which you are familiar, ask yourself the question:

→   Do you sometimes think that changes are needed in the setting?

If your answer is 'Yes', what would you then do about this?

You will need to consider this need for change. You have the potential for leadership in that you could reflect on current practice, think about alternative practice, read about what others have written in relation to your ideas, and then present those ideas coherently to the person in charge of the setting, who might ask you to present your ideas to the other staff for discussion. This overall leader will be interested in your ideas if these fit with the overall values and goals of the organisation, and if the leader considers that your ideas might improve achievement of these shared values and goals while still meeting its legal and moral responsibilities.

In thinking about alternative ways of working you are clearly recognising that your role includes leadership. You may not have the final say as to whether your ideas will be implemented, but you are offering your experienced and informed view about potential changes. Doing this in a way which supports the organisation or setting is more likely to result in a positive response from the leader.

Not everyone who is part of the early childhood workforce will be confident enough to suggest changes, or to take up the leadership opportunities in their role. We hope you will find the chapters in this book helpful for you, so that you can begin to take up these opportunities and gain sufficient confidence to demonstrate some of the qualities of leadership. Jones and Pound (2008: 4) note that leadership influences 'others to improve and enhance children's care, learning and development'. We argue that leadership does not have to be in one direction only, that influencing improvements can occur from the bottom up, from the top down, or sideways (influencing colleagues).

LEADERSHIP AND MANAGEMENT

The terms 'leadership' and 'management' are often used interchangeably, but they have a different emphasis. Many roles combine elements of leading and managing, but it is useful to consider the difference. Whalley (2011b) clearly states the differences between the two. Leadership includes developing a vision and identifying shared values within the team, being accountable for quality, and taking responsibility for the needs of all stakeholders, for example children and families and other staff. On the other hand, management is seen as the effective deployment of resources, for example identifying staffing needs, organising a rota, and making sure that records are kept. Management will also include elements of planning and decision making. Leading changes in practice demands both leadership and management skills.

LEADING PRACTICE

We know from research, for example from the Effective Leadership in the Early Years Sector study (Siraj-Blatchford & Manni, 2007), that strong leadership is a key characteristic of an effective early childhood setting. These authors identified a reluctance to lead within settings, and a lack of qualifications in leadership across the early childhood sector. Our own experiences, and research for this book, have caused us to believe that all practitioners in early childhood settings have the capacity for leadership as part of their professional role and professional development.

In our view, the element of leadership which can be undertaken by *all practitioners* is the leadership of *practice*. Elements of leading practice identified by Whalley (2011a) include: being reflective and reflexive; having knowledge and understanding of children and their development; having knowledge and understanding of learning; valuing the child; and having a vision for practice.

To support leadership of practice, these elements can be incorporated into the development of all early childhood practitioners. For example, each practitioner can be encouraged to reflect on their practice and consider changes to practice. This can be done informally by the practitioner and by others in the setting on an ad hoc basis, but also formally with mentors. Although many starting practitioners will have no or limited knowledge of child development or of learning, this can be built into the development of the member of staff, through induction activities, expectations, reading and sharing in the setting. Valuing the child is an expected 'value' which can be reinforced by the culture of the setting, and as practitioners take this on board they can contribute to the culture, for example through reflection on activities within the setting and how those activities demonstrate the value of the child. A vision for practice is often something new employees have, or they can see different ways of doing things – this is to be encouraged, so that through reflection the need for changes in practice can be identified and planned for. The final chapter of this book considers ways in which we can improve practice through reflection. Activity 1.3 below is intended to support you in thinking about working collaboratively to support developments in practice.

ACTIVITY 1.3: VALUES IN PRACTICE

Esme is a new member of staff who has not worked in an early childhood setting before. She has noticed that the boys seem to avoid the dressing-up corner, whereas the girls play there quite often. When the manager asks her how she is settling in, Esme raises this point.

The manager suggests that Esme finds out more about what the curriculum says about opportunities to dress up, and also finds out what other staff think about this issue. Esme asks the manager if it is acceptable for her to ask the boys about dressing up, and the manager agrees.

When Esme asks the staff they are willing to share their experiences and ideas with her, and also suggest that she brings her ideas to the next team meeting.

→   Who is leading practice in this scenario?

In this example leadership of practice is demonstrated not only by Esme (who sees that something could change) and her manager (who is willing to support Esme to find out more and suggest changes), but also by the other staff who are willing to listen to ideas and suggest a mechanism to discuss those ideas and potentially make a change (the meeting). Discussing issues with the children (as Esme proposes) draws the children into leading development and change within the setting.

WORKING WITH OTHERS AS LEADERSHIP

In early childhood settings we work with children as well as parents, families and carers; colleagues who are assistants, managers, our boss, room leaders, and members of the multi-agency team; the local authority; schools; and other settings. You will be able to identify at least some of these groups of people in relation to your own role. It can be difficult working with other people, but it can also prove rewarding. The early chapters of this book focus on work within the setting, with children, families and other members of staff. Later chapters consider working with the multi-agency or interprofessional team, and across settings. If leadership is enacted in all roles within early childhood settings, then this is likely to lead to effective holistic practice (Allen & Whalley, 2010). The promotion of team and partnership working is essential within early childhood settings, because the setting alone does not form the child's world, and working with those who the child has contact with, or could effectively support the development of the child and family, is an important part of the early childhood practitioner's role.

KNOWLEDGE AND SKILLS FOR LEADERSHIP

We want to encourage you to think about your role within the early childhood sector and support you to develop leadership within that role. A good starting point here is to make a list of what you do and the knowledge and skills you utilise. Try Activity 1.4 now, noting down your responses. You may need to come back to this periodically, as you think of the various other things you do.

ACTIVITY 1.4: WHAT DO I DO? WHAT SKILLS AND KNOWLEDGE DO I USE?

Think about a typical day in your early childhood role. What do you do? Make a list of all the things which form part of a typical day in one column. Once you have done this, write down which skills and knowledge you might be using or might need to develop in another column. For example, you might use communication skills, organisation skills, or your knowledge of development, behaviour or hygiene. There are no right or wrong answers, and you can add to these lists at any time.

Table 1.1 Own Role

Things I do in a typical day	The skills I use or need	The knowledge I use or need

We focus on some particular skills in this book, for example communication, assertiveness and resilience, to support you to develop these skills yourself, or help to develop these in others. By thinking about the skills and knowledge you already have, and the skills and knowledge you need, you can take ownership of your own professional development as an early childhood practitioner (see Chapter 5 for more on this topic).

LEADERSHIP AND CONFIDENCE

One of the benefits you will gain from reading this book will be a growing confidence in the importance of your role, and with that confidence should come the start of a positive spiral of demonstrating leadership. We consider that all members of the early childhood workforce have the potential for leadership in their role, and that using this potential can provide great satisfaction in the daily enactment of that role. We enjoy hearing stories from practitioners in a range of settings about how daily practice has been changed to improve outcomes for children and their families. Many of these accounts of changes in practice demonstrate a commitment to inclusive and collaborative practice. The values of early childhood practice are therefore strongly evident in leadership of practice, a point identified by authors in the field (Jones & Pound, 2008; Whalley, 2011b; Davis, 2012).

The importance of developing confidence has been identified in research by Hadfield et al. (2012) and by Davis and Capes (2013). Early childhood practitioners gain confidence through education and opportunities to engage with making changes to practice. A confident practitioner is one who is more at ease with considering opportunities for change, being pro-active in considering the way resources are used, in communicating with parents, in identifying training needs, and in sharing learning from training within the setting. This confidence is embedded in knowledge about best practice, understanding children and their development, and recognising the importance of being professional. Confidence in their own knowledge enables practitioners to consider the longer term and more holistic view as regards outcomes for children and families.

THEORIES OF LEADERSHIP

This section presents a short description of a number of theories of leadership and evaluates opportunities for their use in the early childhood sector. Trends in leadership have changed over the decades. There has been a general shift from a focus on leaders' characteristics and the traits of a good leader towards more general leadership guidelines, organisational leadership, and the need for transformation and vision.

TRADITIONAL VIEWS

A traditional view of leadership, and very popular in the early days of work on leadership, was the trait or 'great man' theory, popularised by the Scottish philosopher

Thomas Carlyle (1869) in terms of history being largely explained by 'great men'. In the 1860s this was argued against by Herbert Spencer, who focused on the role of society in shaping such 'great men'.

From the perspective of leadership, 'great man' theory assumed that leaders are born rather than made, that leaders are charismatic and lead because of the people they are, that the skills of leadership are relatively rare, and that the traits of leadership are innate. Alongside all this, however, was an emerging recognition that 'good leader' traits could be learned and thus did not have to be innate. There was increasing interest in the trait approach to leadership from the 1940s on in fields such as psychology, looking at the particular characteristics of a good leader. This interest in trait theory declined in the 1970s and 1980s, although there has been some renewed interest more recently, and it continues to have a place in leadership texts (Daft, 2011).

The 'great man' view of leadership has never sat comfortably within the early childhood workforce where the emphasis is on care, compassion, collaboration, and being supportive. The very name given to the original theory, 'great man', disregards the female workforce, and Siraj Blatchford and Manni (2007) state that gender is largely ignored in the wider literature on leadership and management. Those who have identified gender in leadership writing tend to identify women as more participatory and democratic (see Scrivens, 2002, reporting on work by Shakeshaft), and again this does not fit with trait theory. However, Eagly and Carli (2007) have identified that strong leaders' key traits, such as intelligence, the use of initiative and being able to persuade others, are found in women just as much as they are found in men. This focus on traits which can be learned, and which are just as likely in women as in men, is now much more evident in the literature (see for example Bennis, 2009) about leadership traits. Despite the increasing recognition of women as effective leaders, formal training for leadership roles may not be sought out by women and formal leadership positions are not sought out by women as often as they are by men (Babcock & Laschever, 2003; Northouse, 2015). Women prefer to take on informal roles to support leadership.

So what does this mean for women in early childhood settings? The willingness to informally support leadership is very evident (Babcock & Laschever, 2003) and can be encouraged, for example in supporting practitioners to make suggestions for change. Provision of leadership training, for example through informal and formal professional development activities, and recording this training to recognise this leadership for individuals and across the setting, is a useful way of overtly identifying the leadership knowledge and skills within a team. Good use of mentoring can help to identify practitioners' natural abilities as well as their training needs. For example, a new member of staff may need training in assertiveness (see Chapter 3) whereas a more experienced member of staff may need training in supporting positive staff morale. You might find it useful to revisit Activity 1.4 now as you think about your own development needs as a leader. A lead practitioner in our research for this book identified that she fully supported staff development and this occurred in many ways:

'Through daily coaching, and through our performance review system, and supervision meetings, and training, we have different training pathways to support staff, our core pathway for everyone, and a senior pathway for anyone wanting to progress that way, and the leadership and management pathway, so lots of opportunities to access training both internally and externally'.

ORGANISATIONAL LEADERSHIP AND MANAGEMENT

With larger, more complex organisations has come the introduction of more hierarchical and bureaucratic leadership and management systems. These are more impersonal and based on the notion that employees must follow procedures rather than think for themselves. This can be beneficial for large organisations with lots of workers as it can keep control, but workers will often consider they have no voice in the organisation. The recent rise in large-scale businesses which run nurseries nationally and develop policies at a national level means that early childhood settings may be affected by such bureaucratic leadership. This can provide real challenges if the staff values in a setting are not the same as those of the overall national organisation. A successful organisation will recognise the local contexts of its settings, and provide sufficient flexibility for local leaders to implement local policies which reflect the needs of the local community.

The technical-rational view holds that leadership should be confined to certain individuals in appointed leadership roles. Technical-rational approaches emphasise maintaining the status quo. Formal structures are present in the organisation to achieve pre-set goals. For example, specific leadership posts with specific functions and specific authority mean such roles have both power and influence. Leadership is often top-down in this model. For the early childhood workforce leadership of practice is embedded in every role, hence this technical-rational model does not sit comfortably with most settings. However, putting in place specific roles to lead change in practice can have very positive effects, as was demonstrated through studies of the Early Years Professional role (Hadfield et al., 2012; Davis & Capes, 2013).

A range of other leadership theories can be useful in considering the practice of leadership. For example behavioural theories of leadership consider what a leader does rather than who the leader is. Traditionally the leader has been characterised as autocratic and authoritarian, democratic and participative, or laissez-faire in their style (Daft, 2011). In many early childhood settings democratic leadership is appropriate, although this can be more time consuming because greater consultation and communication with the stakeholders is required. Many now have a view that democratic leadership does not go far enough, and distributed leadership is more appropriate for early childhood settings. For example, Jones and Pound (2008: 4) state that 'leadership is ultimately distributed, shared and dispersed in early childhood settings' and there is discussion in the literature about the use of distributed leadership in settings (see for example Heikka & Waniganayake, 2011). In this sense leadership is inclusive of the range of practitioners within a team, who are each enabled to take responsibility for best practice within their role and influence best practice within the setting through professional reflection and positive communication within the team. We consider shared leadership in Chapter 6.

These notions of democracy and shared leadership contrast with the view of leadership as transactional, based on leading a task or getting a job done, which may include rewarding staff for achieving higher targets. Such transactional leadership is often employed in call centres, but does not fit well with leadership in the complexities of early childhood settings.

LEADERSHIP AND CHANGE WITHIN THE CULTURE OF THE ORGANISATION

The idea that leaders need to be able to adapt to different contexts has been present in the literature for some time, with theories such as Fiedler's contingency model and Hersey and Blanchard's situational model (Daft, 2011). More recently these ideas have developed into a more modern institutional view of leadership. This view holds that leadership occurs within a changing environment and that all staff have the potential to lead. Leadership is seen as a *culture*, not necessarily designated to specific roles. Leadership exists in the relationships between people (for the early childhood setting this will include relationships with children, families, other staff in the setting and the wider interprofessional team), so interaction with others is the key. In this model, leadership emphasises the survival of the organisation as it changes and adapts to a changing society and changing demands. Changes in structure and the culture of the organisation are considered against the needs of the community. Different employees at different levels of the organisation can take different leadership roles. This type of leadership values the relationships between stakeholders (for example employer, employee, children and families, local community), group decisions are encouraged, and staff are involved and empowered. Influence can occur upwards and downwards. The model assumes a socially relevant organisation with links between the outside world and the internal world of the organisation. The culture of the organisation is developed in relation to its social relevance.

There are some elements of this model which sit very well with the early childhood workforce. For example, as leaders we want to ensure the culture of the setting matches the espoused values of the team, and supports children, families and staff in contributing positively to the setting. Also, because an early childhood setting does not exist in a vacuum, but as part of a community, changes in national and local policy will reflect the need for changes in settings. Strong early childhood settings with a culture of leadership embedded within all roles will be able to support changes while working for the integrity of the setting within its community.

TRANSFORMATIONAL LEADERSHIP

More recently, ideas about transformational leadership have been evident. Although the term 'transformational leadership' was used by Burns as far back as 1978, ideas about this theory have since developed. These focus on the necessity of the leader having a new and clear vision, and being able not only to see the need for change but also to explain to stakeholders the purpose of that change (Northouse, 2015). Such leaders will need to motivate others in the organisation by engaging with all stakeholders both cognitively (so that they understand the change) and emotionally (so that they want the change). When major change is needed, transformational leadership can be very useful. Transformational leadership is particularly necessary to consider when the culture of the setting needs to change. A word of caution though: it is possible as a leader to get carried away with such a model, and ignore the values of shared leadership.

Theories of motivation linked to leadership are certainly not new, but as a component of transformational leadership theory they are worth noting. Earliest of these was Maslow's (1943) hierarchy of needs. This theory suggests that unsatisfied needs act as a motivator, and once the need is satisfied, another need becomes a motivator. Staff who are asked to work in an environment which is too cold, and where they are unable to take appropriate comfort breaks, are likely to be poorly motivated because their basic needs are not being met. At the top of the scale of needs are those of self-actualisation, where creativity is encouraged as a motivating force within the job role. There are many criticisms of Maslow's theory, but despite these there is value in considering the theory. Other theories of motivation include Adams' (1965) equity theory, which states that people are motivated if they believe they are being treated fairly. In early childhood settings, having open communication and opportunities to discuss issues within the team can support a sense of fair play.

Consideration of motivation is useful for the leader in early childhood settings. Working with someone who is demotivated can have a strongly negative influence on others in the workforce, and can make work challenging rather than enjoyable. On the other hand, employees who are motivated tend to want to make the setting the best it can be, and will be more likely to suggest positive actions to improve things. Locke (1968) proposed that agreeing specific, relatively stretching goals can be used to motivate staff who are unmotivated, by focusing their attention on the job to be done. For example, setting a goal for a member of staff to find out about a topic and share this with the team at a meeting could make that member of staff feel trusted with a worthwhile and new task, and could also help them see learning and sharing as part of their role.

Work by Davis (2012) indicates that for early childhood leaders one theory of leadership is not enough, that these leaders draw from a range of theories to support their practice across the range of situations and activities which occur in early childhood settings.

REFLECTION POINT: LEARNING FROM LEADERSHIP THEORY

Based on the outline description of theories above, jot down your ideas about which elements of these theories you might find useful in your own practice.

THEORY TO PRACTICE

You may have included some of the following ideas as part of your reflection:

→ I can learn to be a leader, I don't have to be born with leadership skills.
→ I can identify the skills and knowledge I need to be a leader, and make a plan to develop these.
→ Developing knowledge and skills within my job role will give me confidence.
→ Leadership traits are not gender specific.
→ A culture of leadership in a setting where everyone sees themself as having a role in leading supports a strong setting.
→ Setting specific but stretching goals can help to motivate people.
→ Major change, such as a change of culture, may need transformational leadership.

As a key person, you might be interested to identify the skills and knowledge you wish to develop in relation to your leadership role working with specific children and families. As a room leader, you may identify a need to learn more about motivating staff and leading change. As a new member of staff, you might need to learn more about the curriculum and ways of working with children to lead their learning. Whichever role you occupy, you have probably realised by now that it is our belief that leadership is for everyone.

In Chapter 6 we develop these ideas of leadership and extend them to specific theories about leading change. These elements will be particularly useful for the person who is in overall charge of the setting or has responsibility for a number of settings.

Just before we end this chapter we wanted to point out that the role of the leader should be a positive one, namely to influence best practice and optimal outcomes for children and families, however poor leadership practice can have negative consequences. Work by Einarsen et al. (2007: 208) considered the concept of 'destructive leadership' and the way in which poorly constructed leadership can reduce staff morale and weaken team effort, limit opportunities for staff development, and reduce opportunities to work together with families to promote best outcomes for children.

Padilla et al. (2007) considered the notion further and identified that destructive leadership ignores or does not seek the views of others and hence is not collaborative. A destructive leader will impose targets without discussion, and without consideration of the specific abilities or aptitudes of the practitioner. Clearly, this type of leadership is not ethical and has no place within the early childhood sector. However, Padilla et al. (2007) go further in their article, recognising that for destructive leadership to succeed typically there will be followers who are susceptible to such destructive methods. Practitioners who lack self-confidence, a knowledge of their legal rights or understanding or awareness of the values of the early childhood sector may not realise that this type of leadership is unacceptable. Empowering practitioners, developing their assertiveness and confidence, will therefore mitigate against the potential for destructive leadership. A strong leader will put in place mechanisms to empower individual practitioners to speak up to ensure the best outcomes for children and families.

We hope, therefore, that you will realise the consequences of failing to enact positive and constructive leadership in your role. Leadership can be a powerful tool for improving outcomes for children and their families, but failing to enact such leadership could have significant negative consequences.

SUMMARY AND CONCLUSIONS

We agree with Jones and Pound (2008: 4) who recognise that 'everyone in early years care and education needs to develop their professional knowledge and skills and adopt a leadership ... approach'. Working as a practitioner within an early childhood setting you will be involved with at least one of the following elements of leadership: leading a child in their learning; leading within a whole setting; leading within a room; being a key person; leading across many settings; leading people; leadership with parents and families; leadership with other professionals; reflecting on leadership.

We have identified within this chapter that there are many theoretical approaches to leadership, and that practitioners can draw from these approaches where they fit with the setting. Leadership involves people, so much of what is written within this book is about working with others, namely children, parents, other staff. We hope we have convinced you that everyone who works in a setting has scope for leading practice.

RECOMMENDED FURTHER READING

We recommend that you explore the video material, and research findings, from the EYPS study to see how different practitioners enact leadership in their roles:

Hadfield, M., Jopling, M., Needham, M., Waller, T., Coleyshaw, L., Emira, M. and Royle, K. (2012) *Longitudinal Study of Early Years Professional Status: An exploration of progress, leadership and impact: Final report*. London: Department for Education. Available at www.gov.uk/government/uploads/system/uploads/attachment_data/file/183418/DfE-RR239c_report.pdf

2

LEADING CHILDREN IN THEIR LEARNING

CHAPTER OBJECTIVES

→ Consider the ways in which practitioners can take the lead to support children's learning.
→ Consider how practitioners can support children's development of leadership skills.

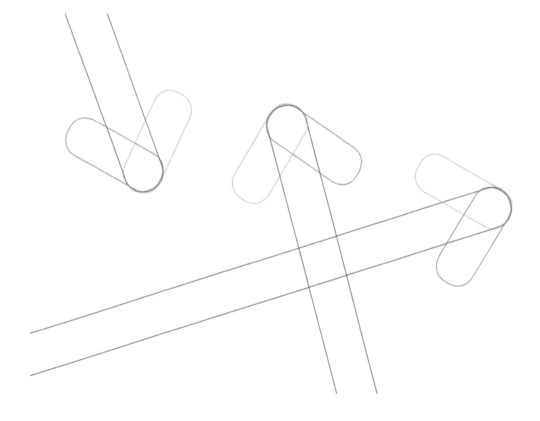

INTRODUCTION

This chapter will focus on two key themes: how practitioners lead children with their learning and how children can be supported in developing their own leadership skills. Within these concepts we shall explore how practitioners can work in partnership with children, as a means of ensuring that provision reflects their needs and interests. Additionally, we shall determine the roles that encompass leading children and how these fit within the Early Years Foundation Stage (EYFS) framework.

Children are at the very heart of early childhood care and education, and virtually everything practitioners do revolves around delivering high quality provision to support them with their life-long learning journey. Over the past few decades not only has the early childhood sector seen sweeping changes and a growth in services, quality and funding, but also attitudes towards children have shifted. There is a greater focus on children's rights and participation, with growing recognition of how children can contribute to provision and develop effective partnerships with their educators and service providers. Developing leadership skills in young children is currently an under-researched area, with a keener interest in children aged five years and above. While the premise of this book is exploring leadership within a professional context, it has also produced an opportunity to investigate whether leaders are supporting young children in developing leadership skills and how this supports learning and development.

OBSERVATION, PLANNING, EVALUATING, REFLECTING AND ASSESSING (OPERA) LEARNING

Before we explore the role of the adult and its implications for learning and development, we first need to look at the tools and methods used to build a holistic picture of the child's world and their personal background. Across the early childhood sector, there is the expectation and requirement to observe the children in our care and then record and assess their progress, in line with a range of learning outcomes and areas of development (Palaiologou, 2012). Leaders are therefore tasked with tracking and reviewing not only children's learning and development but also their own. The EYFS has contributed to improving outcomes for children and raising the quality of provision, with appropriately skilled and well qualified practitioners being integral to this process (Tickell, 2011a; 2011b).

Observation, planning and assessment are fundamental in supporting children's learning and developmental needs, with early childhood leaders using this information to communicate any learning needs to parents, colleagues and other professionals (Department for Education, 2012; 2014b). Two further elements, which integrate with these methods, are evaluation and reflection. Both provide valuable insights regarding how practitioners can take an individual child's learning forward, and address their own pedagogical skills, by ensuring they can adequately provide the resources, expertise and knowledge needed to facilitate learning.

This model for practice, comprising all five of the aforementioned components, has been abbreviated in this chapter as OPERA, as we feel each element complements the other and plays a critical role in addressing past, present and future implications for learning and achievement. There are many books available that focus on specific techniques and methods relating to observation and planning processes, and we would recommend that you take the time to learn more about the various approaches and techniques to enhance your knowledge and understanding. Our focus on OPERA is to provide you with a background regarding its purpose and how this links to both leading learning and developing leadership skills in children. It is important to understand the individual role of each of the aforementioned components as well as how this is used in combination with the others.

Observations act as a starting point within the observation, assessment and planning cycle, as they provide us with background information regarding the child and their interests and abilities, particularly when little information exists (Palaiologou, 2012; Brodie, 2013). When new children start at a setting, leaders are reliant on the background information provided by their families to supply them with some information about the child, including their interests, health and wellbeing, additional needs and previous attendance with another early childhood provider. Information alone does not necessarily build an accurate picture of the child's learning, development and interactions. Children respond differently in an early childhood setting compared to when they are at home or in another social environment. Observations allow practitioners to consolidate the existing knowledge they have on the child and build on this by recording that child's interactions, not just with adults and children, but also with the resources, activities and facilities they provide. Knowing and understanding a child's past, present and future learning feeds into planning and on-going assessment, allowing leaders to explore how they may best support that child's progress.

One significant challenge that may impede the ability to successfully observe and assess a child's progress is where the practitioner and child may have difficulty relating to one another (Bruce et al., 2015). There may be numerous reasons as to why this may occur, ranging from difficulties with attachment, practitioners lacking skills and knowledge when working with children who have additional needs, and even a clash of personalities. In these cases, reflection can play a supportive role in exploring what can be put in place to ensure that leaders have access to acquiring the information they need to support the child in question. This could mean that a new key person is appointed if the child has another adult that they have formed an attachment bond with. It is important that leaders keep children at the heart of any interventions or decision-making processes, and are confident in adapting their practice to meet each child's needs.

What the practitioner observes makes a valuable contribution to planning and assessment procedures. Furthermore, it provides opportunities that enable children to further their learning. Bruce and colleagues (2015) state that the aims of planning should be to take the child deeper from where they currently are, rather than always moving onwards and upwards. Touhill (2012) describes deep learning as a state where children are absorbed, fascinated, active and involved. These experiences provide a richer learning environment and pave the way for children to rethink, discuss and reflect on their learning. When supported by an adult who is genuinely interested in what they are doing, children are more likely to contribute their thoughts on their achievements and difficulties, pertaining to the activities they are engaged with (Smidt, 2005). This type of feedback has two functions: firstly, it allows the child to be an active participant in the observation, assessment and planning cycle, and secondly, the practitioner can use this information to develop further activities that match the child's needs and interests. Evaluation and reflection are not just aimed at supporting learning and development, they make a broader contribution to determining whether the services, resources and curriculum being delivered are appropriate and effective (Ang, 2014).

Observations and planning have historically been used to inform practice within early childhood, and the addition of the EYFS has made it a statutory requirement to assess children and take into account their individual needs, interests and stages of development (Department for Education, 2014b). Developments relating to neuroscience, child development and children's rights have also culminated in a shift regarding the way in which they are cared for and educated. Furthermore, the role of the family is key in providing us with richer content in terms of what a child can achieve or has achieved and what they are working towards. Children will behave differently in different environments, so whereas a child in the setting can appear introverted, they may be an extrovert in their own home. Planning is an on-going cycle and therefore combines what has been observed with the extra information and observations that parents and carers provide. Other professionals and colleagues may also play a pivotal role in planning and assessment cycles, particularly if the child is being supported by other services, such as speech and language therapy and a Special Educational Needs Coordinator (SENCO) (Smidt, 2009). The role that other professionals play in supporting children and families is explored in more depth in Chapter 8.

Our research revealed that planning, observations and assessments varied across the sector, and were dependent on the roles, responsibilities and pedagogical philosophies being undertaken. For example, nannies reported that their planning incorporated day-to-day activities such as mealtimes, play dates and domestic tasks. In comparison, practitioners working in settings that followed Montessori, Reggio Emilia or Forest School approaches would combine their own specific pedagogy with the requirements set out by the EYFS. Steiner Waldorf settings would also engage with observations and planning, although their ethos and approach to learning mean that they are exempt from some aspects of the EYFS, namely literacy, numeracy, technology and some assessment regulations (Steiner Waldorf Schools Fellowship, 2013).

Our research showed that there was a mix of child-initiated and adult-led provision, which differed depending on the age group worked with. Generally speaking leaders working with preschool and primary school children would provide more directed activities, as a means of preparing them for school or supporting them with their studies, that is, reading and spellings. For younger children, planning provided them with opportunities to become independent and develop relationships with adults and other children. For most leaders the way they planned also varied, with many using spontaneous events as opportunities for learning. Langston and

Abbott (2005) stress that planning should be flexible and flow with the child, with practitioners writing what was planned in retrospect. For our interviewees, many activities derived from day-to-day interactions and activities that were guided by the child, with the adult scaffolding learning when the opportunity arose.

Throughout our interviews there was clear evidence that evaluation and reflection were key in determining how practitioners and professionals could further support children's learning and development. Through their observations and planning numerous questions arose which fed into on-going assessment procedures, providing valuable information regarding each child's strengths and areas of learning that required further development (Curtis, 1998). Carr (2001) adds that activities promoting problem finding and problem solving act as assessment sites to determine children's learning dispositions in terms of their ability to take an interest, persist with difficulties and uncertainties, communicate with others, and take responsibility. The role of reflection allows leaders to explore their own pedagogical approaches and consider how the information acquired through OPERA can inform further learning opportunities. In Chapter 9 we consider how this can be achieved through individual and group reflective practices.

Perhaps the biggest challenge in completing OPERA are constraints on time due to juggling day-to-day practice and administrative tasks. Brooker et al. (2010) state that the demand for paperwork is deemed excessive by those working in the sector, with Mohammed (2014) adding that the EYFS has failed to allocate practitioners sufficient time to complete paperwork, stressing that this impacts on opportunities to reflect on practice and provision. Tickell's (2011a; 2011b) review of the EYFS noted that practitioners felt obliged to keep large amounts of paperwork as evidence of on-going assessment. It was recommended that practitioners spending too much time writing and documenting should review their practice, but is this feasible considering the greater focus on accountability?

Developments in technology, such as the use of digital cameras and tablet devices, have produced new ways to record observations and assessments, which could potentially reduce the time taken to document children's learning and development. The advantage of using such devices means that photos can be added to different portfolios, for example in group observations, and this can evidently save some time. Additionally, having learning journals online makes these more accessible to parents who wish to track their child's learning and development, but may not always be available or able to speak directly to a practitioner or key person (Bruce et al., 2015). Amelia's interview revealed how her setting uses email to engage with parents, particularly families who have separated or have a severe medical condition, which affects their ability to visit the setting on a frequent basis. Technology ensures that these families can be contacted and updated regarding their children's progress and provided with an opportunity to contribute information and feedback. There are some disadvantages in relation to using technology, notably not all staff having adequate levels of knowledge pertaining to information and communications technology (ICT) and not all parents having access to the internet. It is important that staff are fully trained in using apps and software appropriately and understand how to store digitally acquired information safely (Piper et al., 2013).

ACTIVITY 2.1

Write down how OPERA is/would be demonstrated within an early childhood setting or your workplace.

→   What information is collected/evidenced for each component of OPERA?
→   How is this evidence used to inform learning in the setting and home environment?

THE ROLE OF THE ADULT IN LEADING LEARNING WITH CHILDREN

As with leadership in other contexts, leading learning comprises a broad range of skills, roles and responsibilities to ensure that the environment, resources and adults support the needs of each child (Curtis, 1998). Our research was comprised of practitioners with a wide range of qualifications and a mix of long-term and short-term expertise across the sector. Regardless of their position or level of responsibility in the setting, there was clear evidence that each person was leading children with their learning. For those trained at a lower level, they referred to their role in terms of supporting and encouraging children and promoting independence. For practitioners with higher level qualifications and long-term experience, their responses were more detailed, with many making reference to theoretical approaches such as scaffolding, constructivism and schemas. Senior staff and lone workers clarified how they would share their expertise and good practice with practitioners and professionals from within their setting or across wider networks. This was seen as important in jointly addressing problems and difficulties in practice, by reflecting on and exploring alternative approaches. In Chapter 6, we shall continue with this subject by looking at some examples of leaders working collaboratively with other professionals from within the early childhood sector.

ACTIVITY 2.2

Consider how a practitioner leads children in their learning:

→   What qualities or characteristics does a practitioner require?
→   How would a practitioner know that they are effectively leading?
→   What could be the barriers or challenges in leading young children?
→   What strategies could be used to address these barriers or challenges?

Consider your responses to these questions as you read through the remainder of this section.

Throughout our research, we asked ourselves how leadership differs when working with children compared to adults. There were three key roles emerging from the interviews which practitioners and professionals adopted when leading learning: Facilitator, Role Model and Educator. The following sections explore each of these roles in more detail.

THE FACILITATOR

Through our own research we discovered that leading learning comprises other roles and skills that complement the leadership aspect of provision. One of these roles which is often undertaken is that of the facilitator. The Elementary Teachers' Federation of Ontario (ETFO, 2011) stresses that facilitation is about guiding rather than controlling the learning that is taking place. Hewett (2001) adds that the educator works in partnership with the child throughout the learning process. Rather than just observe, they play an active role in provoking learning at appropriate times. Good facilitation requires practitioners to structure the learning environment and provide resources and experiences that will enable the child to explore and investigate (Curtis, 1998; Lyford Jones, 2010). Facilitation therefore plays a significant role in providing children with a voice and means of participation. Coleyshaw et al. (2012) and Kanyal and Gibbs (2014) explain that the use of observation, reflection and planning provides practitioners with an understanding of how children are participating, and if children are engaged in the process this raises self-esteem and involves them in decision-making processes.

Practitioners from our study integrated this knowledge into their own practice as a means of tracking children's interests and schemas. Furthermore, they engaged in sustained shared thinking, using it as a tool to prompt children and extend their knowledge and understanding. In many cases this was done in a facilitative capacity, as practitioners were mindful about providing opportunities and space for children to discover and explore independently. ETFO (2011) refer to this as the informed participant, in which practitioners balance being uninvolved with controlling experiences. Rose and Rogers (2012: 70) articulate that facilitation 'demands the distribution of power and control in the pedagogic relationship'. This is seen as something that requires some skill, as much is to do with the timing as to when adults should become involved and when to let the play be self-directed.

THE ROLE MODEL

It is important for practitioners and professionals to recognise and understand how their attitudes, behaviour and actions inform their interactions with children and families. Young children are particularly susceptible to verbal and non-verbal messages and may perceive positive and negative interactions as a cue to behave or respond in a particular manner. Acting as a positive role model is an integral part of working in early childhood, particularly in cases where the family are unable to undertake this level of responsibility. This may be in cases where parents and carers have experienced their own difficult upbringing and may be unsure about how to provide an alternative experience for their child. Other factors, such as illness, addiction, mental health and domestic violence, may impede on a parent's ability to act and respond positively (Moylett & Djemli, 2004). Practitioners recalled how they would partake in an activity, such as tidying up and through active engagement. They felt it was necessary to demonstrate basic skills to children which would support them in becoming more independent. As discussed in the OPERA section, these aspects of practice were often conducted as part of unplanned activities, but what if a child is introduced to a new, unfamiliar or challenging activity? In such cases the leader would demonstrate and model the skills and attributes required, providing a supportive and encouraging learning environment.

THE EDUCATOR

A clear message that was evident in the responses from many of the participants, related to their perceptions of themselves as 'teachers'. While they acknowledged that they did not have the same level of status as a teacher working in a school setting, they emphasised their key role is providing education for the children in their care. Nannies additionally referred to the educational aspect of their role, which complemented the caring duties they had to engage with. The children's participation was viewed as a high priority, as leaders sought to provide them with rich and stimulating learning opportunities. For those working with older children provision was differentiated, giving them more autonomy and a say in decision-making processes. Listening to children and their views and needs was used as a means to determine where they were with their learning, and provided leaders with an opportunity to reflect on their responses and consider further opportunities for learning. James and Prout (1996), Clark et al. (2003) and Kanyal and Gibbs (2014) acknowledge that children are increasingly being seen as active rather than passive bystanders, and listening and consulting with them allows their views and thoughts to be taken into account, particularly when shaping provision.

> 'One day we asked the children if they would like to go on a trip; so we gave them leaflets of possible places we could get to on a coach. So we went through and explained to them and then they would have a vote, so they understood if they put their hand up they were saying yes and if they didn't then they weren't voting for it. So children voted to go to a farm, so I said, "Okay, you would like to go to a farm. How are we going to get there?" So then the children debated, "Well it's too far to walk, we can't bike, we need a coach." Then one of the children said, "Well if we need a coach, we need money, so we will have to pay for that," and I said, "Okay, we are going all day." Another child said, "We will need food," and that led to talk about what they would have, and what they would put in the packed lunch; so they very quickly took control of planning the trip." (Colette, Manager, discussing how young children shaped their own learning experiences through participation)

Providing opportunities for children to lead needs to take into account whether giving extra responsibility is appropriate for a child's level of development and understanding. As this example demonstrated, the manager facilitated the session and worked in partnership with the children to develop a plan for a day trip. Allowing children to share power and responsibility with the adult requires a lot of reflection, in addition to weighing up the pros and cons and any potential risks and benefits that may accompany this level of participation (Shier, 2001). Our final section will explore how children can develop leadership skills and the implications this has for learning and development.

REFLECTION POINT

Reflecting on your answers from Activity 2.2, and comparing the roles of facilitator, role model and educator, which roles and characteristics do you feel you identify with the most? How would you adopt the other roles and use them in practice?

CHILDREN AS LEADERS

Participation and leadership are complementary to one another, as they provide children with opportunities to contribute to provision and equip them with a sense of ownership. You may ask why it is important to develop leadership skills in children this young and question the impact this has on relationships with adults. Leadership is associated with prosocial behaviour and is a means of developing a more positive sense of citizenship. The term 'prosocial' relates to positive responses and interactions in a social environment, where children demonstrate empathy, cooperation, helping and sharing (Denham, 1986; Eisenberg et al., 1999). Fukada et al.'s (2001) study observed the activities and situations in which children demonstrated an array of leadership behaviours. These behaviours included giving directions for the rules of play, suggesting new play ideas, encouraging others, giving permission to join play, considering other children's safety during play, and inviting and encouraging children who were not originally participating or included in games. Educational environments provide a natural setting for children to explore and utilise different leadership skills, and their social interactions are key to supporting this important area of development (Scharf & Mayseless, 2009). If you are working in an early childhood setting, it is very likely that you will have observed children taking the lead during some form of activity.

Early childhood settings are diverse environments, providing young children with numerous opportunities to play and learn in a safe and nurturing environment. As previously discussed in this chapter, leaders play an integral part in facilitating learning and this includes equipping children with the skills needed to support them later in life. According to Lee et al. (2005), early childhood leadership has primarily been studied as part of research focusing on peer acceptance, aggression and adjustment rather than a standalone subject. Our research for this book has also drawn attention to leadership studies focusing on children aged five years and above, with little indicating leadership skills in children below this age.

Practitioners may see leadership skills demonstrated all of the time, but may not necessarily recognise them. This is because leadership is not just about 'being in charge', it is a more complex concept encompassing a wide range of additional skills.

If we look at the guiding principles in the EYFS, there is evidence of the skills and dispositions that are integral to developing leadership skills. These relate to confidence, independence, resilience and self-assurance (Department for Education, 2014b). Observation plays an integral role in recognising these skills and providing learning opportunities and activities to demonstrate and develop them within various contexts. The types of leadership style children use closely mirror the approaches adults use in practice. For example, children may undertake an authoritative role in role-play, make-believe play and group games, implanting their own rules, rewards and consequences. Children who behave in this manner are likely to take control, and may find it difficult to accept resistance to or the rejection of their ideas and games.

Other children may undertake a more participatory or democratic approach, where there is evidence of cooperation and attempting to address problems together. They may take the initiative to create their own games and activities with little guidance from an adult. Babies as young as six months can also demonstrate leadership skills through constructive play and the way they can influence. As children age their leadership style becomes more diverse, with some undertaking a diplomat or adviser stance and others demonstrating more domination and directional approaches (Hillman & Smith, 1981).

In Smilansky's (1968) study of socio-dramatic play, she noticed that in cases where leadership was taking place, the teacher's role was primarily used as a means of settling differences of opinion, as the children were able to devise their own solutions to conflict themselves. It should be noted that the children in Smilansky's study were aged between three and five years, whereas children below the age of three may well need more adult guidance and encouragement to facilitate and scaffold the skills they are learning. Murphy (2011) adds that this particular age group work on communicating their wishes and influencing others, and developing the emotional intelligence that is increasingly needed at this stage, as a means of supporting children in 'reading' others' emotions.

Our research participants were asked how they supported children in developing leadership skills and their responses closely correlated, regardless of their role and the type of setting they worked in. Four key themes emerged from the interviews, relating to what practitioners and professionals do:

→ Developing independence.
→ Providing encouragement.
→ Developing confidence and self-esteem.
→ Providing choices in a range of activities.

It was stressed that opportunities for young children were dependent on their age and stage of ability, with activities closely modelling what a child could realistically participate in. For practitioners working with older children, namely preschool and primary ages, there was evidence of them acting as role models for younger children and scaffolding their learning. This would include showing younger children how to use equipment properly and teaching them new skills. Such opportunities empower and value children, having a significant impact on their self-esteem and confidence. Furthermore, it was evident that the children wanted to lead others and have responsibility. Providing the smallest of tasks, such as counting the number of cups to place on a table or helping to tidy up, was seen as a significant learning opportunity. Leadership was never imposed upon the children, which then allowed them to make a contribution when they were ready and willing.

So what else can leaders do to support the development of leadership skills in children? Hillman and Smith (1981) discussed three areas to guide this process. Firstly, they recommended educators reflect and evaluate their own leadership styles and their levels of sensitivity in response to children's behaviour. This is an important stage as children's and adults' leadership styles may vary greatly, so it is necessary to understand the pros and cons that each approach can have, and use this knowledge to address any potential clashes and conflicts. The second stage centres on developing an environment that encourages self-direction and independent judgement for some part of the day. This is where practitioners may want to review provision to ensure that they are providing child-initiated as well as adult-led activities. Planning and evaluation can assist this and explore new and alternative activities that will support the guiding principles of the EYFS. Finally, children should be provided with opportunities to acquire and enhance skills related to leadership.

For this third stage, we can refer to a study by Lee, Recchia and Shin (2005), which highlights how social skills contribute to leadership. They recognise the role of the educator as a valuable asset in helping children develop decision-making, reflective and communication skills. The prime areas of learning in the EYFS, that is, communication and language, physical development and personal, social and emotional development, act as foundations for building relationships, curiosity and enthusiasm for learning (Department for Education, 2014b). The example below denotes how this may be applied in practice.

> 'I think that when we are doing a project for example, we will often ask the children what they're interested in and what they would like to know. It does give children the opportunity to put their ideas into the group and to steer the project in whatever way it is going. That's very good for those children that have got natural leadership skills and are naturally quite vocal, but I think it's important always not to forget the children that are not like that, so it's about encouraging them and listening and talking to them in other ways'. (Valerie, discussing how children develop leadership skills using Reggio Emilia and Montessori approaches)

Experiential learning provides children with an opportunity to engage in a positive learning environment and explore and use these skills. This is where role-modelling and facilitation can be of use, as the early childhood leader can support children with developing conflict resolution skills and resilience, and engage in sustained shared thinking to address problems and challenges and explore potential solutions. As Scheer and Safrit (2001) explain, the building blocks for future leaders are comprised of self-awareness, social interaction and decision-making skills. As we have discussed over the course of this chapter, children are developing a range of skills through various experiences that practitioners plan and implement as a result of their observations and knowledge of each child. It is vital that practitioners recognise how these skills can be nurtured and supported, through the provision of rich learning environments and their own pedagogical knowledge.

SUMMARY AND CONCLUSIONS

Leading learning is comprised of utilising a wide range of skills and attributes as a means of engaging with and supporting development. Early childhood leaders use observations, planning and assessment to determine where children are with their learning, and this is further supported by evaluating and reflecting on practice and provision. Through our research, there are three key roles that leaders undertake in order to utilise the components that make up OPERA. Facilitation greatly supports the role of the educator, as it determines when the leader should intervene and when they need to take a step back and allow children to experience learning themselves. Role-modelling behaviours and actions is another way of gauging children's interests and scaffolding their learning, and in turn this develops some of the first skills linked to leadership, notably independence, confidence and positive self-esteem.

In this chapter, we have also considered how accountability and expectations can act as a burden, with practitioners raising concerns about the amount of paperwork required to document children's progress. In Chapter 5 we look at the implications this has on leaders' health and wellbeing, and in Chapter 7 we also consider the importance of engaging with families as a means of extending learning and development opportunities. Early childhood leaders play an integral role in leading learning, regardless of their qualification levels and experience. There is scope to consider how young children may also be supported in developing and utilising leadership skills, and the implications this can have on their emotional and social development and lifelong learning.

RECOMMENDED FURTHER READING

We recommend the following texts to further support you in your work with leading children:

Brodie, K. (2013) *Observation, Assessment and Planning in the Early Years: Bringing it all together.* Maidenhead: Open University Press.

Bruce, T., Louis, S. and McCall, G. (2015) *Observing Young Children.* London: SAGE.

Palaiologou, I. (2012) *Child Observation for the Early Years,* 2nd edn. Exeter: Learning Matters.

3

THE ROOM LEADER

CHAPTER OBJECTIVES

→ Discuss the role of the room leader and opportunities for leadership within this role.
→ Consider the use of assertiveness as a component of leadership.
→ Identify ways in which resilience can be developed as a practitioner.
→ Recognise what it means to be an effective room leader.

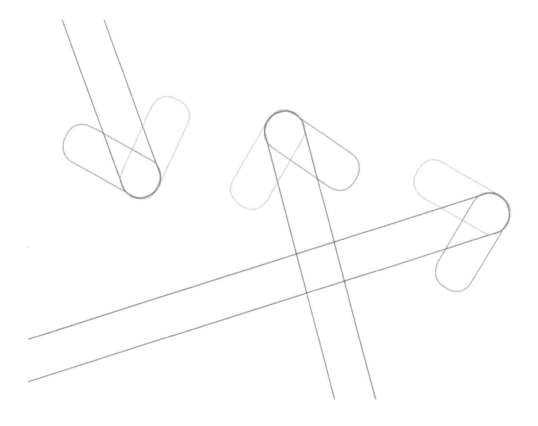

INTRODUCTION

Within this chapter we explore the role of the room leader, and consider opportunities for the room leader to lead early childhood practice. We assume some of our readers will be room leaders, some will aspire to take on this role, and others will line manage room leaders and be looking for opportunities to support the development of leadership within people who work in their settings.

We know how critical certain skills can be in developing leadership ability in this role. For this reason we have included a section about being assertive at work in this chapter. We have also included a section on developing resilience and learning how to influence. Working with others and communicating your ideas is an essential element of early childhood education and care. We all work with others, and being able to consider different ways of doing this to lead changes in practice is a key aspect of this chapter.

THE ROOM LEADER

So who or what is a room leader? There is not a great deal written about the role of the room leader in early childhood education and care settings. Job descriptions are available for the role of room leader in some settings, but in other settings the term 'room leader' is not used, with a preference being given to 'team leader'. The complexity of naming of roles within early childhood education and care has been noted by Nutbrown (2012) in her review of qualifications within early childhood settings. We like the term 'room leader' because it denotes responsibility, within boundaries, for the staff and children, for the planning and activities, for the resources, and for the day-to-day management of a small environment.

In what ways can a room leader show leadership? In her book about quality in the early childhood sector, Helen Penn (2011) identified that practitioners should not be 'technicians' who carry out actions which have been determined by others. In other words, early childhood practitioners should not just follow procedure, they should do more than this to strive to improve outcomes for children and families. We are not suggesting here that following procedure is in any way wrong, we are, however, advocating that the early childhood practitioner should understand the rationale behind the procedures they follow, be able to reflect on their effectiveness, and make recommendations for change. Individual early childhood leaders, including room leaders, can develop their awareness of opportunities to lead practice. The need to develop this awareness of leadership in various early childhood roles is supported by other authors, for example Aubrey's (2011) review of Scrivens' (2002) New Zealand study of female ideas about leadership. In this chapter we are trying to raise awareness and explore the ways in which room leaders can enact leadership. This draws out an important aspect of self-leadership. It is essential to consider the job you do, and to think about how it can best be done, for you and the staff you work with, the children and their families. While policies must be adhered to, they must also be interpreted within your own context and role, the children in your care, and your creativity. Being a room leader provides you with an opportunity to consider different ways of doing things. Becoming a reflective practitioner can support you with this role, and we would ask that you refer to Chapter 9 to further develop your reflective practice.

ACTIVITY 3.1: THE ROOM LEADER'S ROLE

Spend a couple of minutes jotting down what you think the role of the room leader is.

→   What do room leaders do?

Some of your ideas may be about activities which all the staff in an early childhood setting might be expected to undertake. Others might be ones which are about leadership. The list below includes some activities which have been identified as the role of the room leader in job descriptions. We have not listed all the activities, just some of the ones that we consider include leadership. Compare your list from Activity 3.1 with the list below.

ROOM LEADER ACTIVITIES

→   Take responsibility for leading a room.
→   Ensure that high quality practice is embedded.
→   Plan activities.
→   Role model high quality practice.
→   Support staff within the room to ensure high quality care, which may include mentoring staff.
→   Work as a member of a team.
→   Work in partnership with staff and trainees.
→   Work in partnership with parents.
→   Build positive relationships.
→   Keep up to date with current issues about early childhood education and care.

These activities suggest the room leader is an experienced practitioner. Typically a room leader will have at least two years' experience working with young children and that experience is invaluable on many levels. For example, the room leader will have gained experience of working with a range of children and families and a range of other members of staff. They will also have gained understanding of the curriculum, and how this might be planned for and enacted in settings for the range of children in their care. Chapter 2 included examples of leading children with their learning, and much of that chapter is very relevant to the role of the room leader. The purpose of this current chapter is to consider leadership when taking responsibility for leading a room, which can include leading learning, leading staff, leading on use of resources, and being creative in ideas to support these leadership elements of the role.

It is always useful to think about a role in terms of the opportunity it provides the role holder, not just the requirements of the role. The next activity encourages you to do this.

ACTIVITY 3.2: OPPORTUNITIES FOR LEADERSHIP

Read this short case study based on an example provided by a room leader during our research for this book. Think about the opportunities that the room leader has within her role based on this vignette. Names and nationalities have been changed to protect the identities of those involved.

Laura, the room leader, explained that she had introduced some changes over the last year. Within the setting there were children with parents from many different countries. She had been thinking about how best to support these children and gave me an example.

This concerned a little boy who was Polish, but his family were saying he was refusing to speak Polish at home. The parents wanted their son to learn English, but did not want him to lose his Polish heritage. Laura explained that she had planned a themed week about Poland so the child could bring things in to share, such as special memories and links to home. Over the course of a week he taught other children in the room various phrases and how to count in Polish. Laura explained that instead of feeling embarrassed by his difference from the other children, he felt proud. Since then she had included activities about different countries on a regular basis, and these had been introduced across the setting. For example, a Hungarian week was planned, with a mother coming into the setting and reading a story about Hungary.

I asked Laura what had motivated her to make the changes, and how she had gone about introducing these. She described that her motivation had come from a discussion with the parents, and that she identified a need to be more inclusive to support the child to accept his own identity. Laura had explained her ideas to the practice leader for the setting and had been supported to discuss these with the rest of the team and the families. She was also encouraged to try the new ideas. She was required to include her own reflections and those of the team and the families to consider the success of the changes. This formal reflection was standard practice within the setting. Because of the positive feedback, the ideas Laura had introduced were extended to the whole setting.

There are a several examples of opportunities to show leadership in this scenario. Firstly, you might have identified that Laura appeared to have a positive relationship with the parents, so that she was communicating effectively with them, and they had brought an issue to her attention. This positive relationship is vital, and recognises that each child does not solely exist in the early childhood setting, but may have a very different life outside the setting. Rather than dismissing the issue raised by the family, Laura realised that they had a real concern and showed leadership in considering how best to support both the child and the family. Laura appeared to have a good understanding of social and emotional development as well as inclusive practice, and she used this to develop her ideas for the change. Leadership was again shown by Laura in her confidence to discuss ideas with her manager, the team of staff in the room, and the families of the children in the room. Making the changes had a positive effect on the child, and Laura was able to reflect with the staff and with the families about the effectiveness of the change (we explore the use of reflection in Chapter 9). This relatively small-scale change led to a positive change within the whole setting.

LEADING A BABY ROOM

One of the areas in many settings is the baby room. Authors such as Goouch and Powell (2013) have written extensively about practitioners working with babies, and much of this is based on research they have carried out with practitioners in settings. They discovered that early childhood practitioners who work in baby rooms are often seen as 'functional' by others in the setting, and often display behaviour such as 'helplessness' and 'voicelessness' (Goouch & Powell, 2013: 21–2). In other words, the practitioners in the baby room do not consider that they have any control over their own work, and do not think that their work is valued by others.

Consider the following vignette. As you read this, think about the baby room from the point of view of the babies and families, and the point of view of the different practitioners.

ACTIVITY 3.3: VIGNETTE – CELIA AND SOPHIE

Celia is 17 years old. She has recently started work in the baby room at the setting and is studying for her NVQ Level 2 qualification. The setting has 40 children altogether including six babies. Celia started work at 7am and it is now 11am. Her shift is due to finish at 4pm.

The room leader enters the baby room and finds Celia changing a baby's nappy while chatting to another colleague about a trip out she had the previous weekend with her boyfriend. The colleague, Sophie, is 18 years old, and has been in the setting for three months having gained her Level 2 qualification last year. Sophie started work at 8am and is due to finish her shift at 5pm. Neither Sophie nor Celia have had a break today – they normally have a 30-minute break at lunchtime, but cannot take this break at the same time because of staffing ratio requirements.

The room leader shouts at the two practitioners, telling them off for chatting to each other about their social lives, and then leaves the room.

→   Consider yourself firstly in the role of Celia, then of Sophie, and then in the role of the room leader. What are the leadership issues in this scenario? How might you demonstrate leadership in each of these roles?
→   If you were a family member of one of the babies in the baby room, what would your expectations be of the practitioners in the baby room?

There are a number of leadership issues in this scenario. Goouch and Powell (2013) identified that leaders should not assume practitioners will show mothering behaviour just by being with babies. Yet the babies' family members will usually expect that mothering behaviour to be evident for their child while in the setting. Goouch and Powell (2013) found that practitioners may have a lack of understanding of what is required, and also a lack of understanding about the significance of the relationship between practitioner and baby, and the importance of communicating with the baby. As a room leader, the initial induction of staff will need to be considered. Staff need to understand the importance of social and emotional development and their role in promoting optimal development. The room leader here has a personal responsibility to lead by role-modelling good practice. She also has a responsibility to discuss induction and staff development with the manager of the setting, so that a change in procedures can be initiated.

More than this, the scenario does not provide a sense that the setting's values are being enacted in a positive way. There is a need for room leaders to develop a sense of 'value' for the work in the baby room, both on the part of the practitioners in the room and the other practitioners in the setting. The vignette suggests that the least experienced staff have been placed in the baby room, with a lack of mentorship within the role. The setting manager and room leader will need to consider implementing schemes for mentorship, as such schemes can provide ongoing support for staff and have a positive effect on children. In this case some responsibility could be given to Sophie to role model effective practice to Celia. All early childhood practitioners, even the most junior ones, need to be encouraged to take pride in their professional role.

As a room leader it may be helpful to consider the daily routines in the baby room, from the point of view of the babies and from the perspective of the practitioners. Goouch and Powell (2013) found that many practitioners are unable to take breaks during the shift, and this is something the room leader could consider. These researchers also found that practitioners in baby rooms valued sharing their experiences with others, and this sharing, while initially about routines and resources, extended to more sophisticated considerations of roles and ways of working as the research project continued.

The room leader therefore has opportunities to consider ways by which they can enable staff to place value on their role, while at the same time demonstrating the value they have for their role. In this vignette, telling staff off is not helpful. As a leader you would want to change behaviour, and you would do this through influence. Communicating with the practitioners about the importance of their role with the babies and their families is necessary. Providing them with responsibility, for example giving responsibility to Sophie to explain to Celia about attachment, health and hygiene, communicating with babies, is likely to engender a sense of professional responsibility. The practitioners need to access a knowledge of child development at this early stage of life to understand the importance of emotional and social interactions, and not just physical care, for babies. Also essential here is communicating with the practitioners to find alternative ways of working to support them in their roles, for example ways in which they could share their experiences of working in the baby room with others and therefore also share learning. But some way of enabling social interactions between the staff is also necessary, and establishing guidelines for this within the setting is necessary.

BEHAVIOURS AND INFLUENCE

As a room leader, you will have opportunities to influence staff, parents and children. The work of the early childhood leader involves people, and as Rowland and Birkett (1992: 2) comment, 'success at work ... depends on the impression we make on others'. Within this section we consider ways in which to develop assertiveness, learn resilience, and exert our influence over others. Underpinning this section is our belief that early childhood practitioners are professionals, with professional values, ethics and judgement.

BECOMING ASSERTIVE

Assertiveness and aggression are sometimes confused. Bond (1987) identifies assertiveness as a clear alternative to aggression, highlighting that aggression, and manipulation, are strategies which do not respect the rights of other people. In Chapter 7 we explore how leaders may deal with aggressive behaviours when working with parents and carers. Valuing others is an important and fundamental aspect within early childhood education and care settings, and therefore aggressive behaviour does not fit with the values of early childhood settings. Have you ever been on the receiving end of aggressive or manipulative behaviour? Can you remember how it made you feel? Examples of aggression might be seen in someone who shouts, or has a loud penetrating tone, demands, blames, threatens, attacks, gives orders, forces their own view on others. Valuing others means not shouting at them, not trying to put someone down, and not behaving in a pushy and paternalistic way. Valuing others means listening to their point of view, speaking clearly but without raising your voice, respecting the fact that we are all different, treating others as equally of value, and expecting to be treated in the same way. Within this section are a number of activities which we hope might support you in being assertive. Some of them will be more relevant to you than others, so use these as you need to. The overall effect of using the activities should be to enhance your interpersonal skills.

Respecting others' rights is fundamental to working in settings, but so is respecting one's own rights. Many staff in early childhood settings appear passive or submissive, but submission does not respect one's own rights. Are you submissive? Or do you know someone who is? A submissive person may use phrases such as 'I am sorry but ... '; 'I am afraid that ... '; 'Would you mind if ... '. These phrases suggest someone lacking the right to an opinion. You might also recognise a submissive person by the way they regularly back down in an argument or put themself down. A submissive person may moan about what is wrong, but not take positive steps to make things right. And a submissive person may say 'yes' when they mean 'no'. And then they will feel resentful or angry or that they have no power. It can be quite difficult to work with someone who is submissive, because you may not be able to find out what their views really are about a work matter. Passivity in the workplace is not often helpful, and opportunities to move from being passive to being assertive may need to be sought. As a room leader you will need to be assertive by sharing your ideas, communicating effectively with staff, children and families, and being quite clear about what you mean by high quality practice. If you are always passive and submissive, don't expect to change overnight – seek help, and gradually introduce changes. In the activities here there are some fairly practical suggestions. You can learn to be assertive, and improve your sense of self-worth, and you can support others to do so too. This is a vital component in the professionalism of an early childhood workforce. Try Activity 3.4 now.

ACTIVITY 3.4: BUILDING YOUR CONCEPT OF SELF-WORTH (OR SUPPORTING SOMEONE ELSE TO DO THIS)

Step 1 – *Think about your strengths, your abilities and skills, about what you can do well.* For example, are you a good communicator, are you good at sensing when a child needs attention, are you experienced at working with parents, are you creative, are you someone who can bring out the best in others, do you have a sense of humour? Jot down these strengths, abilities and skills.

Step 2 – *What do other people say your strengths are?* You may not yet be confident enough to ask them, but think back – have other staff given you compliments for a job well done? Have you had any comments from parents about what they value about you? Have the children indicated what they like about you (the way you tell a story, the way you make them laugh)? Add these to your list of strengths.

The lists you have jotted down are the basis of your self-worth. You can add to these at any time. Starting with a list will enable you to focus on what you are doing well, and you can take pride from this. Learn to take compliments when someone is positive about something you have done, for example with a response such as 'I was pleased with it too' or 'Thank you, I liked the way it turned out'. These are key steps in developing confidence, and practising being assertive can help to further develop that confidence. Here are some tips which you can use to develop that assertiveness:

→ Think about your *posture* first: have an assertive posture by facing the other person directly, at an appropriate distance, and at the same eye level if possible. Many authors on the subject (for example Rowland & Birkett, 1992) suggest standing tall, upright, head held high.

→ Make *eye contact*, but don't stare, instead try to be relaxed. Do you use hand or facial gestures which demonstrate you are submissive, for example looking down, or fiddling while talking? Think about these and aim to gradually reduce your use of these.

→ And now *the way that you talk*: ask for something you want, but be specific, be gentle but firm, be direct. You are important, and if you do not ask you do not recognise you are important. Remain calm and repeat your request, politely but firmly (there is more about communication in Chapter 4). It can be easier and more fruitful to be direct, to ask for exactly what you want, and to not beat about the bush by moaning about what is wrong. And think also about how you respond to others' questions – be positive rather than apologetic.

To be an effective room leader you need to have self-worth, to recognise what you are good at and value this. But having this self-worth will also help you do your job by allowing you to identify others' strengths. Rather than seeing one person as better than another, an assertive individual will recognise the range of strengths within the team. By finding out and recognising what you are good at, you can see that you are not inferior to your work colleagues. You need to develop to a position where you can take both positive and negative criticism, and accept blame if it is due, but where you will not accept unfounded criticism and blame for blame's sake.

The next activity supports your development of assertiveness at work. It presents a number of triggers and asks you to consider an assertive response to these, for example by using a set form of response or 'script'. We suggest that you draw from the ideas in the section above, and also from the 'script' suggested by Rowland and Birkett (1992). The script is presented below, and shows how it might be used by a room leader who has been told off in front of parents by the manager:

1. State the behaviour which is occurring ('when you told me off in front of parents').
2. State how it makes you feel ('it made me feel small').
3. Empathise with the other person ('I understand you were angry').
4. State what you want to happen ('if you want to express your anger, please don't do this in front of parents').
5. Provide a choice ('if you insist on telling me off in front of parents I will be obliged to insist that we remove to a separate place to communicate').

ACTIVITY 3.5: BEING ASSERTIVE

Here are some hypothetical situations to help you think about ways in which you could be assertive. How would you respond assertively in each case? Draw from the 'script' suggested by Rowland and Birkett above. Have a go with the following triggers. We suggest that you make notes as you go through each one:

Trigger 1: Manager to practitioner – 'Jenny I have told you I will not have you spending time with parents at the end of the day, get them out and we can go home'

Trigger 2: Practitioner to another practitioner – 'Jan will do it, she likes to be supportive'

Trigger 3: You have asked for confirmation of the working schedule for the following week, and the response from the manager is 'I will let you have that on Friday, I have told you I am too busy now'

Trigger 4: You hear gossip about a colleague, for whom you have respect – 'You know I really do not like that woman, I am sure she has it in for me, she asked me to be polite for goodness sake, what's wrong with a few carefully chosen swear words?'

Did any of these triggers remind you of situations you have experienced? Here are some suggestions in relation to each of the triggers given above.

Trigger 1: As an early childhood practitioner you value the time with parents, and know it is an important mechanism for linking learning between home and the setting. To respond assertively you can state the value of spending time with parents, and also state that at present there is no other time to do this. You can ask how things could be changed to ensure there is time for parents. You can also suggest how a time for parents could be built in differently within the session. For example, your response might be 'At present, we do not have a time to talk with parents, and communicating with parents is important. I feel I am not being professional if I do not communicate with the families. I understand that we need to lock up at the end of the day and finish on time. I would like there to be a time when communication with families can take place within the day. If there is no other time for communication with the parents, then I will have to continue to communicate with them at the end of the day'.

Trigger 2: This trigger suggests that Jan always says yes, and also suggests a rather derogatory view of Jan from her colleagues. There is a difference between being a willing and supportive team member, and being someone who is taken advantage of. In this scenario, Jan might want to consider whether or not she wants to do what is being suggested. She may want to practise this using phrases such as 'I am pleased you think I am supportive, and I agree with you, but on this occasion someone else will need to undertake the task'.

Trigger 3: This trigger suggests that the manager lacks understanding of the needs of her staff. It is a reasonable request that is being made, so it would seem reasonable for you to be assertive in requesting next week's rota. You could make statements such as 'I understand you are busy right now, but I need to know the rota so that I can arrange my own schedule. Could I please have the rota for next week before the end of today?' Or if there is a policy in place you might wish to refer to this, for example 'I know you are busy, but we agreed on a policy for notice of the rota for the following week'.

Trigger 4: Gossip can be problematic and generate challenges for effective team working. Being professional means treating colleagues with respect. A difficulty with a colleague is usually best taken up initially directly with the colleague. Moaning about a colleague to others is not being assertive, it shows a lack ability to tackle a situation in an adult way.

An assertive person will be able to speak about their own views comfortably, while still respecting those who may have alternative views. The early childhood workforce is caring, and sometimes being assertive can be equated to being uncaring. However a truly caring individual will want to speak up for the child or parent or colleague and be an advocate when required. Equally, being assertive can suggest that this might lead to individuals not liking you, so it is important not to personalise things if you ask someone to do something and they refuse. Being assertive suggests that you have a right to express an opinion, it means you do not rely solely on someone else to take the decisions, and it demonstrates that value is given to a variety of opinions.

All the room leaders we interviewed for our research identified that assertiveness was a key element of their role. This assertiveness included the confidence to role model to children and other staff, and also set clear boundaries within the room concerning what was acceptable behaviour. Being confident enough to role model positive behaviour is important to room leaders and they consider that this has a positive effect on children's learning. One room leader in our research summed up the assertiveness required in their role as follows:

> 'If someone hasn't pulled their weight, just ask them, see if they need support, keep positive, don't blame, give support, find out when it will be done rather than assuming it won't be done. So be supportive as a team. If we see something that isn't best practice, be open, make suggestions as to how to do it better next time. We have mutual respect, we listen to each other'.

LEARNING TO BE RESILIENT

Taking control and being assertive require resilience. This section considers the elements of resilience and some strategies you can use to support yourself to learn resilience. Some of these strategies will be very useful in a range of roles you may occupy, early childhood practitioner, parent, leader, mentor, to name just a few. Becoming resilient is empowering, it moves practitioners from a feeling of powerlessness to a feeling of strength.

In this section we want to draw on a very interesting study of teachers' resilience in disadvantaged South Australian schools in which their mechanisms for coping with stress were explored. The study describes some of the highly stressful situations that teachers were exposed to, including aggressive and non-concordant behaviour from parents and children, and physical and verbal abuse. Howard and Johnson (2004) identified evidence of a range of strategies which demonstrated the teachers' resilience in these challenging circumstances. These included:

→ agency;
→ having a strong support group;
→ being competent and having a sense of achievement.

Teachers demonstrated a sense of agency as a 'strong belief in their ability to control what happens to them' (Howard & Johnson, 2004: 409). This is contrasted with a sense of 'fatalism or helplessness' (2004: 409) which would equate to a lack of control. Teachers' sense of control of a situation included choosing to not to feel guilty when stressful situations presented themselves, and not to see the event as being their fault. The teachers had learned ways by which they could 'depersonalise' (2004: 410) events rather than taking things personally. In addition, they described learning from situations when they could have done things differently rather than feeling bad about what had happened. Furthermore, the teachers tried to understand the behaviours of the parents or children, in relation to the circumstances these parents or children found themselves in. Howard and Johnson (2004: 410) use the term 'moral purpose' to reflect the choice that teachers had made to work in these challenging schools, and the sense of agency was enhanced by their drive to 'make a difference' (2004: 411). The findings from this study demonstrate a real sense of self-belief in the teachers, a belief in their own ability and an assertiveness in their role. Now consider the study's findings in relation to your own role using Activity 3.6.

ACTIVITY 3.6: RESILIENCE AT WORK

To what extent do you have a sense of agency in your own work? That is, do you think you can control what happens at work, or do you think you are helpless and cannot make a difference? Look at the two sets of statements and decide which of these most applies to you.

Set 1

→ I often blame myself when things go wrong.
→ I often feel guilty when things go wrong.
→ I take things personally if a colleague or a parent or a child has a go at me.
→ I am helpless, there is no way I can influence anything.

Set 2

→ If things go wrong I realise that it is not necessarily my fault that this has happened.
→ There is no point in feeling guilty, it is better to find out what happened and learn from what went wrong.
→ If something doesn't work, I will reflect on why it didn't work and do it differently next time.
→ I can make a difference at work.

The first set of statements in Activity 3.6 suggest a feeling of helplessness, a sense that the person has no power within their role. The second set of statements suggests self-belief and a feeling of self-worth – a feeling that your actions are important in supporting positive outcomes within your setting. This consideration of where you think you fit now can help you identify ways in which you can move to having a greater sense of empowerment within your role.

Within the study by Howard and Johnson (2004), the teachers had mechanisms to support their sense of agency. They all described strong support mechanisms both outside the work environment (from family and friends) and within the work setting from other staff. Support within the work setting included not only discussions with colleagues but also strong support from the leadership team, and a sense that the team believed in the teachers' ability and professionalism. You might find it helpful to consider the opportunities that present in your setting for discussions with colleagues. You might also like to consider the ways in which practitioners are trusted as able, professional individuals. Such considerations might lead you to make changes to your own practice as a room leader. Chapter 9 in this book supports reflective practice, and one of the activities asks you to consider the extent to which you have a supportive team. Being a strong team can clearly be important in generating a sense of agency, a sense of being able to make a difference.

A further element of resilience was identified in this study (Howard & Johnson, 2004). The teachers' own knowledge and skills in the work that they had to do, and their belief in their knowledge of strategies of how to deal with challenging behaviour, provided them with confidence and a sense of their own ability as well as a belief that they were doing an important job. As a practitioner, thinking about the skills and knowledge you already have, and what you need to develop, is an important part of setting the course for your own professional development. Look back at the list of room leader activities at the start of this chapter. Are you fully equipped for the role of room leader? If not, make a plan to develop those areas of knowledge and skill which will enable you to do the job more effectively. Some of this you can do informally through reading and discussions with others. But you should also discuss your development needs with your manager so formal opportunities for that development can be taken.

Another element which emerged from the Howard and Johnson (2004: 415) study was the teachers' beliefs that they had 'learnt' to be resilient through their experiences, reflection, and being mentored. This is very encouraging – the teachers did not consider they had been born to be resilient, they had learned to be resilient. We would encourage you to consider your own resilience, and the extent to which you can improve this using reflection on practice and the support of colleagues, as well as being mentored by a more experienced practitioner.

THE EFFECTIVE ROOM LEADER

Thus far we have considered the role of the room leader and the activities this role might include, some examples of the way in which leadership can be enacted in the role, and a discussion of the behaviours required to support leadership and influence practice in order to become an effective room leader. Earlier in the chapter we identified that a room leader's role included taking responsibility for leading learning and leading staff, for being creative and using resources effectively. As one of the room leaders in our research stated, 'I see myself as a leader ... leading the children, and the staff in the room'. We now explore these ideas from the experiences of the room leaders we interviewed during our research. We provide examples from our research with early childhood practitioners about what it means to be an effective room leader.

The room leaders we interviewed were very clear about their role in leading children's learning. They identified planning and being aware of individual children's needs and level of development as important aspects of leading learning. The room leaders (based in England) identified the importance of the Early Years Foundation Stage as a basis for planning activities within the room as a whole and for individual children. As one room leader stated, 'you have to understand that children won't learn in a rigid style, you have to adapt to meet all the needs of the children'. The room leader, with the key person, will plan learning for individual children based on their interests and level of development. The activities are also planned by the room leader so they can be accessed by several children at different levels of development and with varying needs. The room leaders identified the importance of role-modelling for children, both to learn behaviour and to learn specific skills.

Communicating with families about children's development is essential here, in order that there is the flow between home and setting, and the room leader is expected to show leadership with parents. Discussion with parents about what has taken place in the setting, and what has taken place at home, is a vital part of promoting this flow between home and setting for the child, so that learning in the setting can be continued at home and vice versa. Families may also value support if they are facing difficulties with their children at home. One room leader described how she had a child who could follow the 'golden rules' of behaviour perfectly in the nursery setting but would 'play up' at home. In this instance the room leader created a leaflet for all the families about how to work with their children to promote the golden rules at home.

The room leaders also identified mentorship of new staff as part of their role. In some cases apprentices were employed in the setting, requiring close mentoring to enable them to understand their role. In other cases the mentorship related to the new members of staff who were supported to understand the values of the setting and the policies and procedures related to it. One room leader, in describing her work with a new apprentice, stated 'basically I role model best practice, so she can observe me and how I interact and work with the children, and explain what I am aiming to do, and how it links to the EYFS'. Within this same setting we found evidence of a strong culture of staff development. New members of staff were supported with planning and their role as a key person. They were encouraged to observe more senior members of staff in the room, but also learn through doing and reflecting on their actions. Reflection took place with the other staff in the room as well as on an individual basis.

The importance of working in partnership with the other members of the team and with the families, focused on optimal outcomes for each child, formed a strong element of the leadership role for the room leaders we interviewed. The room leaders also identified the need to be creative in their role. One room leader explained how 'inspiration stations' were used by the practitioners to share ideas and support each other: 'We carried out the activities from the child's point of view, gel and cling film on the floor, and yoga, and moving like animals, and cooking and brushing teeth, and sensory tunnel'. In this way, the practitioners gleaned ideas from each other, and each practitioner had an opportunity to devise activities creatively. To find out how useful the activities could be with the children, these were tried out and reflected upon, with the findings shared within the staff group.

In our interviews with room leaders, there was good evidence of the value these practitioners placed on keeping up to date with developments in early childhood education and care. They did this through reading professional and parent publications and discussing issues with colleagues. The room leaders further identified that as new policies and new procedures came into place, these would be discussed within the team to understand the underlying rationale for change and then consider the best ways to implement policy within the local context. Finally, the room leaders were taking responsibility for their own development, identifying training needs and requesting support in the form of mentorship, gaining additional experience within the setting, or attending staff development courses.

SUMMARY AND CONCLUSIONS

Room leaders are confident, assertive practitioners who work effectively with their team to enhance outcomes for children and families. They take responsibility for planning learning, for mentoring and developing staff within the room, and for thinking creatively and cooperatively about the development of learning activities to embed high quality practice. Room leaders are able to use their skills and experience to influence early childhood practice within the room they lead. They are also able to influence practice in the wider setting. Room leaders keep up to date with developments in early childhood education and care. Reflecting on developments within the room they lead, and communicating effectively with the setting manager, enable the room leader to positively influence the development of early childhood education and care practice across the setting.

RECOMMENDED FURTHER READING

We would recommend the following paper which considers gender and leadership:

Scrivens, C. (2002) 'Constructions of leadership: does gender make a difference? Perspectives from an English speaking country', in V. Nivala and E. Hujala (eds), *Leadership in Early Childhood Education: Cross cultural perspectives.* Proceedings of OULU Forum, University of Oulu, Oulu, Finland. pp. 25–32. Available at http://herkules.oulu.fi/isbn9514268539/isbn9514268539.pdf (last accessed 12 October 2015).

4

THE KEY PERSON

CHAPTER OBJECTIVES

→ Identify the role of the key person in supporting children's emotional development.
→ Consider the key person role from the point of view of the child and the family.
→ Discuss the need for emotional resilience in the key person.
→ Recognise the importance of leadership within the key person role.
→ Consider the skill of communication as part of the key person role.

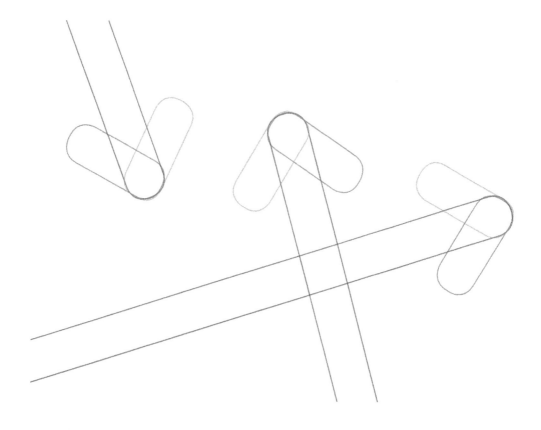

INTRODUCTION

This chapter is about the importance of strong relationships with children and their families. Its focus rests on the role of the key person, and how that role can be enacted through leadership in a way that promotes positive relationships for children, families and members of staff. The significance of the role in the social and emotional development of children is emphasised. We also consider the need for emotional resilience in the key person, and strategies to support this resilience. Attention to the key person role has been re-emphasised in the UK through the Early Years Foundation Stage (EYFS), with the Department for Education (DfE, 2012) guidance identifying that every child should have a key person in a setting. This was based on the findings of the EPPE project (Sylva et al., 2012) which highlighted the key role that adults in an early childhood setting have on the personal, social and emotional development of children.

Working with children as a key person requires strong communication skills. We consider these communication skills in the chapter, and consider ways to use those skills to promote best practice. We have drawn from our research with early childhood practitioners and include the views of practitioners about their key person role.

WHAT IS THE ROLE OF THE 'KEY PERSON' AND WHY IS IT IMPORTANT?

Strong, loving and caring relationships provide the basis for the development of a child's strengths and independence (Allen & Whalley, 2010). In this section we demonstrate that the key person has an important role in promoting these relationships and thus supporting the emotional and social development of the child. Evans (2008) describes key persons as 'lynchpins' of early childhood settings, suggesting that they play a vital part in the setting. This role is considered by some to be particularly necessary for children under three years of age (Allen & Whalley, 2010). Senior practitioners in our research identified that the key person role is more focused on forming secure attachments for the younger children, and also more focused on developing independence for the older children in early childhood settings, while ensuring a sense of security and belonging for all children. This was summarised by two of the participants in the research we undertook for this book who were describing their roles as key persons:

> 'I used to deal with under twos, but just now I have moved to the older children. For the younger children we must focus on attachment, bonding, cuddles, reassurance, feeling secure, but with the older children I try to challenge them; they are more familiar with so-called strangers, they are more forward and will ask your name, so I do encourage them to be more independent, to support them to develop. At the younger end we do challenge them, but we do have to be very sensitive to their emotions, to make sure they feel secure, and not missing their parents too much, feeling secure'.

'I am in the older end, the pre-school end, it has different roles; in the younger room it is a really strong bond, and nurturing, and feeling secure away from mum or dad, but in the older room it is working one to one with children and identifying different interests and any ways the children can extend their learning. About them being an individual'.

In some roles, such as that of childminder or nanny, the idea of the key person has been in place for a long time. Typically a childminder will work in a home setting, with a small number of children, and a family atmosphere is present. The child will feel a sense of 'home' at the childminder setting, while recognising that the setting is not actually their home. The childminder will usually speak with parents on a daily basis when the child is being collected from the setting. Because the setting is small, the childminder will be in a position to know each of the children well, to understand their home contexts, and to form strong and supportive relationships with the children and their families. A nanny will usually live within the family home, and have quite a detailed understanding of family dynamics and the context within which the child lives. They will be able to form relationships with the children and other members of the family within the family home. The nannies interviewed as part of our study described their diverse roles and responsibilities when caring for their 'charges'. Although their practice differs from that of practitioners working in group settings, it closely mirrors that of a key person. They are primarily responsible for observing, monitoring and tracking each child's learning and development, often referring to the EYFS to plan activities and using daily routines and domestic tasks to support learning. They frequently report back to the parents, regarding any issues and achievements linked to learning and development. Furthermore, they act as advisors to parents, providing expert advice relating to both care and education. For those who worked as maternity nurses, they play a key role in supporting new parents develop attachment bonds with their newborn baby. The bond is not just with the child, but the family as a whole.

A practitioner in a larger setting will typically not have this same insight into all the contexts of all the children in the setting. However, enacting the key person role within a larger setting means that individual practitioners will be able to focus on a smaller number of children and their families within that setting. Thus, the key person role enables each child and family to benefit from stronger relationships with practitioners, as practitioners in their key person role will have the opportunity to gain this insight into individual children in their care. In Chapter 2 we considered how the role of the key person is integral in supporting observation and assessment processes, which contribute to effective learning opportunities.

ACTIVITY 4.1: THE ROLE OF A KEY PERSON

→   In your view, what is the role of the key person in relation to the child and their family?

The key person is in a unique position to be able to notice the child, to act to support the child's development, to make observation records, to respond to questions from the child, their family and other practitioners. The key person has an opportunity to communicate with the child, their family, other staff in the setting, and the multi-agency team. Penn (2011) identifies the richness of the conversation that can be had with children when the adult and child share an understanding of that child's context. For example, if the key person has an understanding of the child's family group, the cultural values of the family, and the expectations the family have of the setting, this can support a richer communication between the key person and the child and the family which then better supports the social and emotional development of the child.

It is clearly vital we work to support children and families, and as a key person we have a unique opportunity here. The key person is the identified contact with the child and the family, and it is the key person who has a particular role in the child's social and emotional development, and in communicating with the family and child. To further explore the role of the key person in the social and emotional development of the child, the next section of this chapter considers the concept of attachment, before thinking more specifically about how a key person can work with both child and family.

THE IMPORTANCE OF ATTACHMENT

John Bowlby first wrote about attachment theory in 1958 (Bowlby, 1958). Challenging some of the assumptions in the work of Freud, he identified the very significant emotional bond between mother and child which is evident very early in a child's life. Since then, many have supported or challenged Bowlby's original ideas about attachment, and some of the historic and current views about attachment are presented here. The concept of attachment relates to the strong emotional bond which exists between the child and the child's carer(s). The terms 'primary' and 'secondary' attachment (Bowlby, 2007) are now used to identify bonds with the main carer, and with those who also have an emotional bond with the child. The key person role is based on the value of attachments, which is why the theory of attachment is interesting to consider in this chapter. The key person is able to support the child as a secondary attachment figure, but is also in a strong position to support the family to understand the importance of attachment for the child's social and emotional development.

The theory of attachment suggests that each child has an innate need for an emotional bond based on a need for survival. The primary attachment bond usually forms with the mother, as the main caregiver, but can form with a variety of others, the father, grandparent, carer, for example. Secure attachments are ones in which there is a 'predictable, safe, and affectionate bond with an attachment figure' (Bowlby, 2007: 309), and such attachments are related positively to the social and emotional development of the child not only through childhood but also into adulthood. There is a suggestion that having a number of secure secondary attachments can increase the child's resilience (Bowlby, 2007; McElwain and Booth-LaForce, 2006). This implies that the role of the key person in forming an attachment to a child can positively support that child's development.

A number of psychological studies have considered the characteristics which promote attachment with the child, and an understanding of these characteristics can support the key person to promote both primary attachment (between the child and the main carer) and secondary attachments (for example between the child and the early childhood practitioner). Biringen (2000) has researched the concept of emotional availability, and suggests that attachment is easier if the attachment figure *wants* to form a bond with the child. A parent who is loving towards their child is likely to form a bond naturally. For most parents and carers this love for the child, and a desire to form positive attachments, come naturally, but for some these are more difficult, and an early childhood practitioner can act to support a parent or carer in these situations to work towards a stronger attachment. In Chapter 7 we additionally explore how parents themselves form attachments to the key person, and the implications these can have on transitions and relationships with families.

For an early childhood practitioner, and particularly for the key person, this emotional attachment can be easy, but it can also be challenging, and the section below on emotional resilience considers some of these challenges. In our research with early childhood practitioners, it emerged that there may not be a natural and immediate bond between the key person and the child, but the practitioner through experience can learn to adapt themselves to develop strong supportive bonds to the various children for whom they have key person responsibility. Practitioners can get to know how to support each child. Examples from our research included finding out whether a child needs cuddles, or whether they need more structure to support their sense of security and belonging within the setting. Getting to know a child and their level of development and needs will support the key person in their role as a secondary attachment figure.

There is a considerable volume of research within the field of psychology regarding the concept of attachment. One of the earliest studies was by Mary Ainsworth and colleagues, who developed a way of measuring the quality of primary attachments using the 'Strange Situation Procedure' (Ainsworth et al., 1978). While such studies may be useful in making decisions about interventions to improve attachment, they can also lead to a sense of labelling of the caregiver, a sense that that person is failing the child. As early childhood practitioners, we are more concerned to support positive attachment. Normal attachment behaviours include the development of stranger anxiety, which means that the child is aware of the presence of strangers, and separation anxiety, when the child demonstrates that they do not want to be separated from their attachment figure. These anxieties are often evident when a child first attends a setting, and some of the discussion later in this chapter considers ways to support children and their attachment figures during such transitions.

Neuroscience research (see the literature review conducted by Winter, 2010) has demonstrated the link between social and emotional development and cognitive development. In other words, a child's brain development is directly affected by their social and emotional status. The key person role can support the child's emotional and social development and, by implication, can also support cognitive development. A child who is self-confident and able to form secure attachments will be supported to learn new knowledge and concepts.

We can see from the above discussion that attachment is considered very important. But what if a child does not have the opportunity for attachment? Anning and Edwards (2006: 26) point out that if the care in settings is of poor quality, or 'emotionally detached', children will not form the secure attachments to adults which they need. Evidence from a study by Belsky (1999) in the USA suggests that where there is a lack of attachment, identified as relationships which are detached or inconsistent, children's behaviour and social and emotional development will be affected and could negatively impact on their transition to school. On the other hand, the value of strong attachments is linked by Palaiologou (2016) to positive transitions for the child, from home to setting and later on from setting to primary school.

The Early Education (2012) document *Development Matters* stresses the significance of attachments, and the role of the key person in promoting attachments is emphasised by Bennett and Palaiologou (2016). These authors note the need for a key person to provide 'emotional warmth' (2016: 351) and the importance of stability of relationships within an early childhood setting, with relationships which continue during the child's time at that setting. We are not promoting the key person role here as a primary attachment, as this primary attachment is usually between the child and one or both of its parents, but the key person role does aim to provide a significant substitute attachment.

Our research for this book, with early childhood leaders, identified that practitioners who undertook the key person role were very clear about their role in forming secure attachments with the children in their care. They were aiming to 'make sure the child is reaching their potential'. The practitioners also recognised their role as 'second main carer' and focused on working together as a team of practitioners with families to support their children's optimal development.

THE KEY PERSON AND THE CHILD

The first part of this chapter has explained how necessary the key person role is. In this section, we are mainly looking at the role from the child's point of view. Consider the example below. While you are reading through this, make a note of the main ways in which the child might see the key person.

ACTIVITY 4.2: AN EXAMPLE FROM PRACTICE – MARIA AND JOHNNY

When he first arrived at the nursery at age 2, Johnny was reluctant to leave his mother, clinging to her and hiding his face against her as she tried to put him down in the setting. Maria was identified as the key person for Johnny. With the

(Continued)

(Continued)

agreement of the family, she made a visit to Johnny's home, greeting Johnny's parents as though they were already good friends. During the visit, Maria joined in a game between Johnny and his father while his mother was out of the room making tea. While they were drinking tea, Johnny's parents chatted to Maria and they enjoyed a make-believe game with soft toys which belonged to Johnny.

On the next visit to the nursery, Johnny's mother greeted Maria like a friend, then stayed and joined in the activities. Gradually, over four visits, Johnny came to see Maria as someone his parents knew and trusted.

Now, when Johnny arrives at the nursery he looks for Maria, his key person, and holds out his arms to be taken into the nursery by her. She welcomes him with open arms.

→   How does the child initially view the key person? How does this view change? Why does it change?

This example demonstrates that the child needs someone to attach to when not with their family. They have a need for strong relationships (loving and caring) and these relationships provide the basis of their strengths and independence. Elfer et al. (2003: 84), in their work linking an effective key person role with quality provision within early childhood settings, identify that 'a settled close relationship is forged' and 'children feel safe and cared for'. The example above demonstrates the way in which the key person and family worked together to forge this strong, secure relationship.

We referred earlier to the particular need for the key person role for children under three years of age. David et al. (2003) confirmed the importance of social and emotional development as part of the holistic development of the young child. Goldschmied and Jackson (2004: 41) also identified that 'the denial of close personal relationships is a serious flaw in much group childcare which can partly be overcome by changes in organisation'. They go on to promote the role of the key person for children aged under three. They particularly note that it is not just that a *key worker* should be identified for assessment, observation and organisation relating to the child, but that a close personal relationship is needed to support attachment in these young children, namely a *key person*. This means emotional investment on the part of the practitioner. Goldschmied and Jackson (2004) explain that from the child's point of view, there is a sense of abandonment when they are left in a setting, and the positive relationships with practitioners work to avoid this sense of abandonment and their associated anxiety. In the example above, Maria is investing time and emotion to develop a strong relationship with Johnny and his family, so that Johnny can feel secure in his attachment to her and feel at home in the setting.

However setting up a key person approach can be challenging. From the point of view of the child, there may be an expectation that the key person will be there every time the child attends the setting, and if the key person is not present this could be unsettling for the child. Part of the role of the key person is to work with others in the setting to manage that role. This may include thinking about a system of shared roles, or working within a small team, all of whom become familiar to the child, so that if cover is needed for a member of staff, for example due to illness or to their absence for training, the child will still recognise the staff and settle with them. In this way a number of secondary attachments may be formed with staff in the setting. In our research for this book, we interviewed early childhood practitioners who were in the key person role. These practitioners strongly emphasised that 'the focus is on the child' and that 'they aren't my children or hers, we are open together, we are a team, we communicate with each other'. Thus, the formation of strong attachments was very important, but the practitioners avoided forming exclusive attachments. Instead a number of secure secondary attachments were formed between the child and the practitioners. As an example given by a participant in our research, the key person is often the practitioner who will know a child best in the setting. This key person will be able to assess the child's specific development and pick up on aspects which may need particular attention, for example concerning speech. But the plan for development will be shared across the team, so that whoever is working with the child will be aware of and able to focus on supporting specific aspects of development for that individual child.

REFLECTION POINT

Think about the role of the key person – do you think you have the skill set to undertake this role?

The importance of professionalism in working as a key person came through strongly in our research with practitioners undertaken for this book. These practitioners stated that there had never been situations where they were unable to make an attachment to a child. Rather, they adjusted their behaviour based on the child. As an example, one practitioner indicated,

> 'you change the way you are with the child; if the child enjoys lots of cuddles, you give them cuddles, but some children are not cuddly, they want to get on and do things, so you let them get on with activities, you adjust yourself to suit the child rather than get the child to suit your ways, I just adapt to the child, the extent to which they need me or don't need me'.

Goldschmied and Jackson (2004) provide some very practical suggestions to maximise opportunities for close relationships between the key person and the child. From the point of view of the practitioner, there can be a reluctance to develop a strong emotional bond with a child (Goldschmied & Jackson, 2004). These concerns have a number of elements. There may be anxiety that the practitioner is taking the role of a family member which could lead to resentment from the family. There may be concerns that the child could become too close to the practitioner, or more demanding, or that the practitioner may become too close to the child. Having a close working relationship with the family, and being open in communication of the need for the child to feel secure and loved while not having to compete for that child's affection, are important. In this way, the practitioner will be supporting the family, rather than competing with them:

'Sometimes, parents think you don't know anything and there is another set where they're not jealous but they ... It's almost like they resent ... because obviously we spend more time with their children and I don't know, they just find it hard because obviously they are the main carers and sometimes they have to go back to work. It's not necessarily their choice, but they have a need to go back to work; so we do get some parents who can be a little bit awkward, like to make things difficult just because ... It's almost like a guilty thing, because they've left their child in childcare five days a week, so that can be quite challenging because obviously we don't want to make anyone feel they are not good parents. We just want ... I'm interested in the child and we want to help them to help them, if you know what I mean?' (Amelia, level 3 practitioner, discussing one of the challenges of working with families)

THE KEY PERSON AND THE FAMILY

The role of the key person is not just about the relationship with the child, the key person must also work with parents or carers as partners, because after all, as Elfer et al. (2003; 2012) point out, they are the primary key people. So in some ways it feels as though, as a key person, you are part of an extended family for the child. The family want to be able to trust the key person, to know that that person has their child's best interest at heart, and that the child will be well cared for. This means that a 'genuine bond' (Elfer et al., 2003: 84) will develop between the practitioner and the child and their family. As a key person, you will want to set up positive relationships with the child and the family from the time the child starts at the setting. Knowles (2016) stresses the importance of a home visit, preferably by the identified key person, prior to the child starting at the setting. Our example in the last section included home visits. One or more home visits are likely to promote more positive relationships with parents/carers, as well as starting the process of attachment between the child and the key person. Seeing the home visit as the beginning of the relationship between the setting, particularly the key person, and the parents and child, means that the key person can have a better understanding of the child's context, and the child and family can start to get to know the key person.

Obviously this home visit may not always be possible. And one of the challenges for the key person is that not all families will have the time or the desire for this home visit, and not all settings will be able to organise such a visit. The advantages of a home visit include getting to know the child and the family, and their context. A home visit can be a useful starting point from which to share information about the setting, and also to share the expectations of both parents and setting. It can provide a sense of familiarity before the first visit, and prove reassuring for both the child and the family. The disadvantages are that it takes time, and it may not be possible for the key person to be released for a visit. It may also be difficult to arrange a suitable time if parents are working during the day, and not all families will welcome a practitioner into their home.

When a child starts at a setting, parents or carers can feel mixed emotions, and it can be hard to leave the child in the care of relative strangers. Pileri (2010: 236) identified the 'welcome-separation and reunification' elements within early childhood settings, the points at which a child arrives at the setting, and the point at which they are reunited with their family at the end of the session. Working with first and second generation immigrant families, from a variety of cultural heritages, Pileri identified the range of ways in which parents separated from their child at the start of the nursery session, and the ways in which practitioners welcomed the child at the start of the session. She identified differences based on the security of the parent as a migrant, either as someone who had embraced their original culture within their new one, or as someone who was entirely focused on their adherence to the new culture, thereby denying their original culture. In other words, Pileri's work is emphasising the significance of working closely with parents in order to understand the meaning they give to the relationship between the child and the practitioner. Pileri (2010: 236) discussed the 'musicality' employed as part of the separation period, both on the part of parents and that of the practitioner, describing the use of 'voice, gesture and movements' as part of a ritual to cope with the separation, for the child and for the parent. She emphasises the value of these routines in providing security for the child and the parent. The welcoming routine from the practitioner supports the secondary attachment within the setting, and the leaving routine from the parent supports the parent to let go. The need to work with parents to support a realistic routine for separation is emphasised. If it is possible for the parent or carer to be present at the setting on some occasions before the child is left without them, this time can be useful to reassure parents of the suitability of the setting, and it can also be a useful time in which to role model ways of working with the child to support this separation.

Participants in our research for this book identified the importance of the bond which forms between the child and the key person, both for the child and for the family. In the words of one key person,

> 'the bond is very important, because the parents are giving you their child to look after, the parent wants to feel their child is happy ... if they are happy the child will reach out their arms to you in the morning and not want to stay with mummy or daddy'.

The focus on initiating close relationships as the child starts at a setting is vital. However it is also important to consider the longer term, and the time when a child will have to leave the setting. Thinking beyond the setting, as the child develops and becomes ready for school for example, Allen and Whalley (2010: 87) identify the use of a 'cover system', with the child expecting to interact with different individuals as well as with the key person. Forming secure attachments in early childhood settings can promote resilience in the child, and this is linked to their ability to make successful transitions to school (Palaiologou, 2016). In our research for this book practitioners emphasised the importance of the role of the key person, summarised by one participant as:

'The child will naturally attach; as a key person with a baby you will change their nappies and things, but not get so attached that they won't go to others or go to the next room. They need to gain confidence to move on, to become independent. When they are ready to go to the next room, I will go there, and settle them in, and they gain confidence with the new people'.

Success in the key person role, in forming strong attachments to the children, did not create resentment between families and practitioners for the participants in our research. They were careful not to have 'favourites' and to be open with the families about the bonds between children and practitioners, and also never to undermine the importance of the child's primary bond to their main carer. The key person needs to form supportive relationships with the child and the family, within safe boundaries, but while making provision for building on the child's interests and supporting independence and confidence for them to explore their world. The key person is not the primary attachment figure.

THE REWARDS AND CHALLENGES OF BEING A KEY PERSON: DEVELOPING EMOTIONAL RESILIENCE

In the section above we have identified that forming a close relationship with a child and their family can be very rewarding. Practitioners are in a position to provide 'professional love' (Noddings, 2003) but this is complex, and something which requires experience and resilience within well-qualified practitioners (Page & Elfer, 2013). The emotional aspects of early childhood work are significant and can therefore be challenging. In Chapter 3 we began to consider ways in which the practitioner can develop resilience within their role to support assertive behaviour. We are extending these ideas here with a focus on emotional resilience.

Some bonds between practitioner and child form much more naturally than others. This is challenging because there may be a practitioner in the setting who seems to be the preferred secondary attachment figure for a child, and if a key person has already been agreed it can be difficult for the natural attachment to be ignored. One decision which settings have to make in relation to choosing a key person is when to identify this person, and it may be appropriate to do this once the child settles naturally with one individual. As a practitioner it can seem very hurtful that a child prefers another practitioner. Equally, when a strong emotional bond is formed with the child there is also emotion for the practitioner in the later painful separation (Elfer, 2012).

Thinking through the emotional elements of the work, Elfer and Dearnley (2007) evaluated professional development to support practitioners in this emotional work, and identified a lack of access to training and development about the key person role. Phair and Davis (2015) also noted that even when such development was accessed, that training was not always made use of within a setting.

Practitioners may be wary of safeguarding guidelines and also reluctant to allow close relationships to develop for fear of reprisals. Specific training in the role of the key person and its value is needed, while clearly setting the parameters of the role. Such training should be shared within settings to enable the development of positive secondary attachments through the use of the key person role. This aspect of recognising the value of the key person role is important for the setting manager as they need to recognise and plan for this. They will be able to identify for practitioners the purpose and value of the role. The manager will also be able to provide training in understanding attachment, understanding the boundaries of the role, and developing resilience to professionally manage its emotional aspects. The key person can additionally role model best practice for other practitioners so they can learn about how to support children's emotional and social development in the setting.

The rewards of the key person role are the strong relationships which are formed, not just with the child but also with the family, and the opportunity to impact positively on a child's development and resilience. In our research for this book, we asked practitioners about how they coped with the attachments which form between children and themselves, and especially about how they manage their own emotions when a child and their family leave their care. This element of the role was professionally challenging for practitioners. In one sense, being able to form very strong attachments demonstrated how successful the practitioner was as a key person. The role supports a child to become independent and resilient, and develop their confidence, especially in the year before moving to school. But being able to manage the end of the attachment, typically when the child moved on to begin school, was professionally demanding. The practitioners in our research for this book managed the end of the attachment by focusing on what had been achieved for the child, and the success of their transition to the next phase of their learning and development. The practitioners were able to reflect on the way in which the bond they had formed with a child and their family had developed that child's resilience and independence. The focus therefore was not on the loss of the relationship, but on the successes of that relationship and how those could be used as new children joined the setting. Practitioners described to us their sadness in ending these attachments, but also their sense of achievement at a job well done.

THE KEY PERSON AS A LEADER

Drawing together some of the various elements from the chapter so far, we can identify some of the leadership elements of the key person role. The EYFS links the key person role to leading children's social and emotional development. For the youngest children, the importance of attachment, and forming secure bonds, has been highlighted, to enable these children to develop their emotional resilience. The key person will lead the development of this attachment and sense of security for each child in their care. For older children, once they feel secure within a setting, the key person can lead each child's learning by developing their growing independence and their confidence about who they are.

Another key element of leadership within the key person role is in leading partnerships with families. Getting to know a child and their family, and working with that family to support them in the care and education of their child, requires strong communication skills. Developing positive relationships with families will open communication channels and facilitate open communication. Being able to role model best practice will support a child to settle into their new environment and provide a consistent message to the child that will help them feel secure. Communication from the key person must also extend to other members of the team. It will be these team members who will be there when the key person is on holiday or on a different shift, so communicating their way of working with different children and their families is highly necessary to achieve consistency. Finally, the key person can take a lead in supporting children and families in other transitions, for example from the setting to school.

When we asked practitioners about the most important skill they needed to support their role, they were unanimous that this was the need to be a strong communicator. It is this element of leadership within the key person role that we consider in the next section.

USING COMMUNICATION AND EMOTIONAL INTELLIGENCE TO SUPPORT LEADERSHIP IN THE KEY PERSON ROLE

Communication has many elements, so becoming a skilled communicator can take time. Have you thought about the way you speak to children, colleagues, families? Have you thought about the non-verbal elements of your communication, your appearance (for example, your posture, facial expression, position) when you communicate, and whether your words and appearance give the same message? Have you thought about how good a listener you are? Are you able to reflect on how you communicate, to think about your communication from the other person's point of view, and in so doing improve the way you communicate?

Verbal communication is about the words we use and the way we use them. A message is communicated most clearly when the main part is emphasised and not hidden. But communication is two-way – it is not just about what you say and the way you say it, but also about the listener's ability to hear and make sense of what you are trying to communicate. Developing professional and trusting relationships forms the basis of strong communication at work. Once people get to know you, they will also know whether you are someone who speaks the truth, whether you are someone who is kind and considerate but fair. Families expect and deserve a professional relationship with practitioners, which includes effective communication.

Practitioners who contributed as participants in the research we undertook for this book indicated the importance of experience in learning to communicate. They emphasised that although it was important to learn some of the techniques *from the book*' and practise these outside the setting, learning from more experienced colleagues was essential in enabling practitioners to put effective communication into practice. Being coached by more senior colleagues enabled them to think about how to tackle more challenging conversations with parents. Here, senior staff were able to discuss with more junior practitioners how to structure conversations with families in a positive way, in relation to the specific context of the child and their family. Senior staff draw on their experience with families in many different contexts and with many different needs. All staff are able to collaborate, reflect, and learn from each other to support best practice in communication with families, as identified by one of the practitioners, a key person in a nursery setting:

'I will support the staff, based on what they need, through coaching. We share ideas a lot, I experienced some awkward conversations two or three years ago, I have learned from that, and now team members will come to me to ask how to communicate with the families, and I will guide them based on my experience, and give examples, and then guide them further based on their experience'.

One of the important elements of the communication is for the practitioner to retain their professionalism throughout, rather than moving on to a personal conversation. The key person is in an optimum position to get to know the families of the children in their care, and how they prefer to communicate. For the practitioner, it can be useful to consider how they would like to be communicated with if they were a member of the family.

The next activity considers how to communicate with families in a more challenging situation.

ACTIVITY 4.3: COMMUNICATING WITH FAMILIES

Read the interview extract below, which was provided by a key person (we have called her Amanda) who contributed as a participant to our research for this book.

'I have had a couple of situations and I have had to engage quite sensitively with parents. One child was showing challenging behaviours, and I've been on a couple of challenging/managing behaviour courses, so I have learned about how to promote more positive behaviour through devising a plan. One child I was observing, it was clear that lots was going on at home to influence his behaviour. Even though the parents were worried about him acting in this way, they didn't acknowledge that they had a role. I had to engage with them without blaming them, but giving ideas, role-modelling, maybe if you say it this way, use more positive words and actions, not lashing out, so role-modelling what they could do. We always feed back to the parents anyway, we work in close partnership, have parents evenings, just being able to work in partnership and make sure the parents don't feel like you're blaming them but trying to support them'.

→   In what ways was the key person enabling effective communication in this case?

Amanda, the key person in Activity 4.3, was demonstrating her professionalism in several ways. Firstly, she had recognised her need for professional development in the area of challenging behaviour. She had attended training, which provided her with the knowledge, skills and confidence to devise a plan to promote positive behaviour. Amanda had reflected on the issues, and recognised her need to communicate with the family and support them in recognising their role in managing their child's behaviour. In this example, she had communicated in a positive and supportive way with the family, without suggesting or allocating blame. Working with them to devise a plan, and role-modelling how to manage the challenging behaviour displayed by their child, provided a partnership and a unified, consistent and supportive approach. In this example, the words used to communicate with the family must be non-judgemental and supportive, with an emphasis on the goal of positive behaviour. Being welcoming to the family, and providing opportunities for communication, are clearly evident in this setting.

Goleman (1996) uses the term 'emotional intelligence' as the ability to identify, discriminate between, and use our own and others' feelings to guide our thoughts and actions. In the example above, Amanda was displaying emotional intelligence in understanding that the family had not recognised their role in managing their child's behaviour. Rather than responding critically, she deliberately chose the supportive, collaborative approach to manage her communication with the family. Emotional intelligence can be effectively used to support leadership in the key person role. Reflecting on our own practice enables us to consider whether we are able to separate our own emotions from the emotions being experienced by others, and to do this to support positive outcomes.

SUMMARY AND CONCLUSIONS

This chapter has considered the vital role of the key person in early childhood settings, and opportunities within that role to work with children, their families, colleagues and the wider team to lead positive emotional and social development. We have also considered the challenges that you may face in your role as key person, and supplied you with some essential skills to use within this role to develop your resilience.

RECOMMENDED FURTHER READING

We have two recommended readings for you here:

Bennett, J. and Palaiologou, I. (2016) 'Personal, social and emotional development', in I. Palaiologou (ed.), *The Early Years Foundation Stage: theory and practice*, 3rd edn. London: SAGE.

This is an engaging chapter about the importance of theory and practice to the personal, social and emotional development of children.

Elfer, P. (2012) 'Emotion in nursery work: work discussion as a model of critical professional reflection', *Early Years: An international research journal*, 32 (2): 129–41. Available at http://dx.doi.org/10.1080/09575146.2012.697877.

This article is particularly useful in supporting professional development and a culture of reflection within the early childhood setting.

5

LEADING PEOPLE

CHAPTER OBJECTIVES

→ Consider the role of the leader in leading students, volunteers and employees within the setting.
→ Identify professional development as a mechanism of leadership.
→ Discuss the importance of recognising diversity and supporting employees to fulfil their potential.

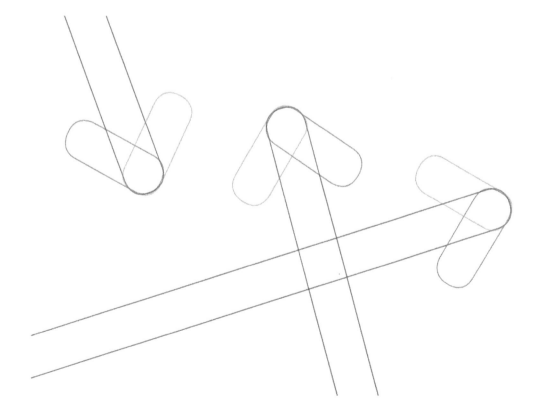

INTRODUCTION

In this chapter, we turn our attention to leadership in relation to working with a diverse range of people who attend the setting in a paid or voluntary capacity. Whether leaders work independently or as part of a group or wider network, we explore the relationships that early childhood professionals have with colleagues, volunteers and students who work directly or indirectly with young children and their families. The first part of the chapter focuses on 'developing professionals', namely individuals who are new to working within the sector or considering a career working with children and families. The second part focuses on professional development for practitioners and leaders, particularly those who wish to pursue higher education studies. The final part of the chapter explores some of the complexities that working with other people brings, such as supporting staff who have special educational needs and disabilities and those who may be affected by mental health conditions.

LEADING 'DEVELOPING PROFESSIONALS'

Early childhood settings have a long-established tradition of hosting students and trainees seeking a career working with young children. For many practitioners progression has come via the pursuit of further training and gaining hands-on experience, often in a variety of settings and different roles. Some individuals may have started their career in early childhood as volunteers, either through work placements arranged by schools or by donating their time to support a local setting. Volunteers have historically played a pivotal role in early childhood through informal or formal roles. In the 1960s, when there was a drastic shortage of nursery provision in England, mothers set up their own playgroups which were dependent on volunteers to donate resources. The mothers and volunteers ran the service and led other parents in setting up similar play schemes (Osborn & Milbank, 1987; Cohen & Fraser, 1991). Nowadays, volunteers may be the parents who help out at their school, playgroup or youth club, or members of under-represented groups, offering a range of skills, talents and expertise (Kahn, n.d; Irvine, 2012). The 'Big Society' initiative, as set out by the Coalition Government, aimed to utilise volunteers as part of a move to provide communities with more power and co-own public services (Woodhouse, 2015).

Within the early childhood sector, radical efficiency projects have used parent volunteers to design and deliver services in their local communities. Goddard and Temperly's (2011) research discovered that these initiatives resulted in strengthened relations between providers and families and led to a reduction in costs. This example demonstrates the importance of volunteering being a two-way, mutually beneficial partnership in which both parties can benefit from the outcomes (Volunteer Now, 2012). Furthermore, there is evidence that volunteers have a positive impact on the learning and development of young children. The United States has run the Foster Grandparents Program (FGP) since the mid-1960s, a voluntary national scheme aimed at placing the over-55s with children and young people who have 'exceptional needs'. Their involvement enhanced children's self-esteem, social skills, emotional wellbeing and language and cognitive skills, and provided intrinsic rewards for senior citizens participating in the scheme (Westat of Rockville Maryland, 1998). Furthermore, the Foster Grandparents often addressed gaps that could not be filled by practitioners, such as acting as interpreters for children and families with English as an additional language or sharing the same cultural background. These two examples demonstrate how volunteers can make a valuable contribution across the early childhood sector.

As a leader of a setting, it can be very useful to consider the skills and experiences which volunteers bring to the workplace, and plan how to use these skills and experiences to best effect. It may be necessary to support other members of paid staff to understand the role of volunteers, and to also recognise the necessity of including those volunteers within the setting's daily and longer-term plans. Some volunteers will need considerable guidance in their role, others may need support to understand the ethos of the setting in the same way that new members of staff would need this. Including the volunteer voice, for example through informal or formal meetings, will enable the setting to draw on volunteers' skill sets more effectively, and benefit from the community network that these volunteers may have.

REFLECTION POINT

To what extent are contributions from volunteers part of the leadership activity within settings with which you are familiar? If you are not yet familiar with any early childhood settings, consider how leadership might support the effective inclusion of a volunteer workforce.

Settings additionally act as a base for the development of future practitioners, who arrive as students from a range of educational institutions. Whether they are studying for specific qualifications such as a National Vocational Qualification (NVQ), Early Years Educator (EYE), Early Years Initial Teacher Training (EYITT) or on work experience, these students will be required to use practical experience to meet their course competencies and develop a range of key skills to support employability (DfES, 2002; CACHE, 2016; DfE, 2015a). Not all of them will be studying courses with Level 2 and 3 qualifications, as a growing number of undergraduates and graduates will also use settings as a means of gaining valuable experience, not just in relation to early childhood and education, but also as part of health and social care training programmes. The Care Council for Wales (2012) advise that participants on work experience are able to spend time in structured and meaningful work and engage in domestic tasks, such as cleaning and assisting with the delivery of services. Leaders, in addition to supervising students, will undertake the role of mentor, which requires them to develop a relationship centred around mutual trust, respect, an openness to learning and developing rapport (Rodd, 2013).

Leadership of those who are students within the setting, but not paid members of staff, is worth planning for. What roles might these students take? How can they practise safely, and be included within the setting? What training and development will they need? Who might be able to mentor them? Later on in this chapter, we shall look at mentoring in more detail, along with other methods and approaches used to support professional development. A good student experience is likely to be one where a student feels part of the team, and begins to live the professional experience of working with children and families, starting to understand and practise the values of the setting, and is able to learn from others.

PROFESSIONAL DEVELOPMENT: TAKING IT TO THE NEXT STEP

Historically, early childhood training was based in further education, with limited opportunities to progress unless practitioners undertook higher education studies in fields such as teaching, midwifery, nursing or social work. Since the 1990s, there has been steady growth in the availability of degrees that are specific to early childhood, and the new millennium has seen the introduction of Early Years Sector Endorsed Foundation Degrees (EYSEFD), New Leaders in Early Years, the Early Years Professional Status (EYPS) which has been replaced by the Early Years Teacher Status, and the National Professional Qualification in Integrated Centre Leadership (NPQICL) (CWDC, 2006; 2010; 2011; NCSL, 2008). All of these courses and awards have paved the way for a new focus on professionalising England's early childhood workforce. This is a far cry from the days when early years was viewed as a 'non-profession', although there is still evidence to suggest that many people fail to understand the nature of the roles and responsibilities undertaken by those working with young children (Rolfe et al., 2003; Lloyd & Hallet, 2010). Our interviewees acknowledged that in many cases parents were unaware of the full extent of their practice, presuming that they played with the children all day. In other cases, families did not always understand the rationale behind the advice or guidance provided. These views mirror findings by Rolfe et al. (2003) and McGillivray (2008) who draw attention to the lack of understanding in relation to professional identities amongst early childhood professionals, due to preconceived misconceptions and stereotypes.

Despite these issues, the opportunity to advance learning has numerous benefits, particularly in relation to developing a higher level of knowledge, confidence, and a positive sense of professional identity (NCSL, 2008; Hadfield et al., 2012; Davis & Capes, 2013). The majority of our interviewees had furthered their learning through higher education, with some currently studying at Master's level. Several interviews highlighted that leaders saw themselves as teachers and part of the education sector, feeling that having a high level of knowledge equated to improving the quality of provision for children and families. This contrasts with Robins and Silcock's (2001) findings, in which nursery nurses did not view themselves as teachers, but acknowledged their role in supporting educational duties. Through our interviews, it has become increasingly evident that many practitioners see themselves as professionals in their own right.

One noticeable challenge, in some cases, is related to colleagues not sharing the same level of passion and interest at pursuing higher level learning or engaging with a particular pedagogical philosophy, such as the Reggio Emilia approach. For managers in particular this was a source of frustration, as some members of their team lacked the vision to progress with their career. Within Chapter 6 we consider ways in which to develop others, as well as ways in which to consider your own development needs, and later on in this chapter we shall explore the role of coaching and mentoring and its implications for professional development.

CELEBRATING DIVERSITY

This section continues professional development in relation to exploring the diversity of adults and young people who come to the setting as paid/unpaid practitioners or assistants. We shall explore how diversity amongst staff can be celebrated and supported, and how their skills, attributes and experiences can be recognised and incorporated into practice. One of the most rewarding aspects of working in early childhood is the opportunity to collaborate with a diverse range of people from different cultures and backgrounds, who bring something unique to the setting in terms of their skills, experience and ideas. The term 'diversity' is described by Jackson et al. (2003: 802) as the 'distribution of personal attributes among interdependent members of a work unit'. As discussed earlier, the people who work with early childhood leaders may come to settings as work experience students, volunteers or apprentices, encompassing a variety of roles ranging from mentoring, coaching, educating, caregiving and advising. These roles are not exclusive to the work undertaken when working with children and families, they also play a pivotal part in the way in which individuals engage with their colleagues. We have already highlighted some of the key attributes volunteers bring to the sector, and practitioners additionally bring a whole skill set to support their practice. For leaders it is important to identify and nurture the talents of practitioners who are either new to the sector or experienced professionals joining a new team.

In relation to cultural diversity, we recognise that some groups are underrepresented, particularly across the PVI (private, voluntary and independent) sector. At the time of writing, statistics revealed that the increase in men has seen little growth between 2008 and 2013, with the number of paid male staff working in full day care remaining at 2%. There are additionally less practitioners from different ethnic backgrounds, although the figures here are likely to be subject to regional variations (Brind et al., 2014). Carrington and Skelton (2003) state that a more representative teaching profession may break down stereotypes relating to gender and ethnicity. Our interviewees came from a range of backgrounds and cultures, with some being multi-lingual or having experience working abroad or across other parts of the UK. These skills were advantageous, especially when working with a wide range of children and families from different backgrounds.

ACTIVITY 5.1

→ Considering your own professional journey, who has supported you in developing
   the skills and experiences required to work within the early childhood sector?
→ What support would you offer someone entering the sector as a novice?
→ What support would you offer a more experienced colleague?

You may have identified particular people who have given you opportunities, believed in you, trusted you, or been available for discussion. You may also have identified opportunities to make use of reflection to identify the skills and experiences you needed. The guidance and support of an experienced professional may also have been something that proved valuable to you. Thus, the support you have identified relates to the needs of yourself, or the particular member of staff, as well as the needs of the setting. This support may include development of knowledge (for example, a better understanding of attachment, or pedagogy, or understanding about child development), skills (such as communication, managing behaviour, assertiveness, resilience) and attitudes. We often think of supporting newer practitioners, and guiding and mentoring them to develop effective practice. Support can also be provided for staff who are more experienced than ourselves by offering suggestions, and volunteering to find out about different styles of early childhood practice, as well as being reliable and trustworthy, and communicating assertively.

During the interviews, early childhood professionals discussed the methods and approaches used to support colleagues and enhance opportunities for learning, development and allowing colleagues to reach their full potential, including novices to the profession. This included the use of observations and feedback to review practice and provide recommendations for further development. In some settings, bi-directional observations were a well-established practice. Newer or less experienced colleagues observed more experienced role models, but also more experienced colleagues observed less experienced members of the team and provided guidance and opportunities for reflection.

A further key component used to support staff development was the use of mentoring, a role undertaken by most of our interviewees to support colleagues and trainees in addition to children and families. One of the leaders interviewed discussed how being on the receiving end of mentoring had supported her transition to working in a new environment.

'She helped me sort of understand the daily routine, because it is very different, very much more child-led. The children get their snack by themselves, sort the lunches by themselves; the way we observe the children, long observations, short observations, so understanding the values that this nursery works by'. (Billie, discussing how having a mentor has contributed to her acquisition of knowledge)

For leaders working in a mentoring capacity, they disclosed the importance of role-modelling good practice and using observations as a means of supporting staff in becoming familiar with pedagogical practice and philosophical approaches. This was particularly significant in settings that followed a specific approach, such as Steiner or Montessori. Furthermore, it became evident that mentoring was not just a tool for advancing professional development. Rose, a Nursery Manager, discussed how she used a mix of mentoring and coaching as a means of addressing the needs of under-performing staff:

> 'We have a coach–coach–consequence format which enables staff to have a chat, have a coach on what they're finding difficult, and we address and document it, and it is part of their appraisal and support documents that we do every month. Again, communication is key, not only on the positives but also when you're facing the negative circumstances as well'. (Rose, Nursery Manager, discussing how mentoring and coaching supports bi-monthly appraisals and staff performance)

Mentoring and coaching, while used interchangeably in this case, actually have very different goals. Mentoring supports practitioners in identifying their personal and professional potential. In comparison, coaching is used as a means of supporting staff in performing more effectively, and works with behaviours such as interactions and working habits. This is based on questioning and listening and is often carried out over a set period of time, whereas mentoring is a longer-term process (Dilts, 2003; Rodd, 2013). Communication and relationship building are essential to ensure that the practitioner and the leader benefit fully. In relation to peer observations and feedback, early childhood leaders felt that these made a valuable contribution to reflective practice, by allowing individuals to explore elements of their practice that required further development. These approaches play a key role in unlocking potential and recognising what individual team members have to offer. It is, however, necessary to ensure that staff are provided with opportunities to utilise their skills and experiences and consider which roles and age groups would benefit the most.

REFLECTION POINT

Are there opportunities in your setting to recognise the diverse range of knowledge and skills which are present within the staff group?

STAFF WITH DISABILITIES AND SPECIAL EDUCATIONAL NEEDS

One area which is currently under-researched in early childhood relates to staff who have a disability or special educational needs. According to the latest early years survey, approximately 1 to 2% of paid members of the workforce have some form of disability (Brind et al., 2014). When we look at other figures, the number of people with a disability in Great Britain is estimated at approximately 11.6 million, with 5.1 million being adults of a working age (Office for Disability Issues and DWP, 2014). Further figures related to individuals who were known to GPs, receiving Disability Living Allowance or were identified at School Action Plus (Emerson et al., 2013). It should be noted that many adults have undiagnosed disabilities or learning needs, so these figures may be much higher. This is likely to be more evident in cases where disabilities are invisible, for example specific learning differences (SpLD) such as dyslexia. For staff and trainees who are working in the early childhood sector with an SpLD or disability, they face a number of challenges which affect day-to-day living as well as professional practice:

> 'The closest thing I can describe ADHD as is that I can wake up one day in the morning and know what kind of day I'm going to have, just basically by evaluating how my brain is working on that day., So for example I can wake up in the morning and become more aware of my thinking and think this is going to be really good day today I can think clearly, I'm focused, and then other days I can wake up and I can't do anything, My brain is not working, it's like realising your brain isn't working how it is supposed to and there is nothing you can do about it and it's quite difficult. The dyspraxia comes into that which is poor memory and poor time management, so one of the difficulties in the teacher training role I'm in, effectively the leadership role, it's that time management aspect and managing the paperwork side of things'.
> (Laura, a trainee early years teacher describing the challenges SpLD has on her practice)

In Laura's case, she was fully aware of her needs and had developed her own coping mechanisms to manage the challenges work and life presented. This included keeping notes to address issues with poor memory and organisation and leading a healthy lifestyle. Working within a team and with colleagues, who may have little knowledge and understanding of specific needs and conditions, is something that needs to be addressed to ensure that all colleagues are provided with a chance to shine and make a valuable contribution to the setting.

Ryder's experience of working with and training staff and students with SpLDs and disabilities allowed her to experience first-hand the challenges and barriers they face when working in settings. Some of the key issues pertained to: a lack of understanding and support from experienced colleagues regarding the needs of practitioners and learners who required additional support; training materials, instructions and resources not being available in alternative formats; and, in some cases, negative attitudes that were overtly focused on what the practitioner or learner *could not do*, rather than what they *could do*. The latter perceptions were predominantly due to heavy workloads, which meant early childhood leaders were unable to devote enough time to audit their provision and make reasonable adjustments. However, these barriers can be overcome with good organisation skills and using research and mentoring as a means of ensuring colleagues who have additional needs can work to their full potential.

Our interviews demonstrated how support was reflected in practice, with Jackie and Alice disclosing that several of their staff were dyslexic. As managers, they agreed with Laura by stating that they felt the biggest challenge for staff with SpLD was the amount of paperwork and report writing that practitioners were expected to complete:

> 'When they have written reports, they will bring these in to the office staff to type them up for them. They shouldn't have to worry too much about their spelling, because it's not going out to parents without it being corrected. If they do notices or things, I have to get a member of staff who can bring it up or write them properly'. (Alice discussing the support put in place for dyslexic staff)

Having an awareness of the needs of all staff and making amendments to policy and practice may be seen as time consuming, but it allows practitioners to feel supported and enables the setting to gain from the positive contributions of all staff. Communication is also key and the role of feedback should not be overlooked, as it can offer reassurance to individuals who may find the roles and responsibilities overwhelming. It is difficult to provide exact guidance in relation to working with staff who have a disability or SpLD, it is very much about considering the needs of the individual and what reasonable adjustments are appropriate in supporting them with their daily practice.

STAFF AND MENTAL HEALTH

The nature of working with children and families can lead to practitioners being exposed to complex and often difficult circumstances, which may impact on their ability to fully utilise their skills and expertise. Chapter 7 will explore in more depth some of these challenges, along with the strategies used to lead and manage the more demanding aspects of practice. In this chapter we aim to recognise and raise awareness of the impact the demands of working in early childhood can have on practitioners' mental health and wellbeing. In Chapter 3 we discussed the work by Howard and Johnson (2004) which explored teachers' resilience when working in highly stressful circumstances. For many leaders, being resilient may be all that is needed to work through the more demanding aspects of practice, but there is a risk that some situations may push professionals to a point where it is difficult to 'bounce back'. In this section, we aim to draw attention to an area which is often overlooked and under-researched in early childhood practice, namely mental health.

Since the introduction of the Equality Act 2010, it is unlawful for employers to ask job applicants questions about health or disabilities until they have been provided with a conditional job offer. At this point the questions would relate to whether the candidate meets the employer's health requirements and would determine whether reasonable adjustments to support the employee would need to be made (Government Equalities Office, 2011). While some challenges to mental health are caused by underlying conditions, such as depression, bi-polar disorder and post-traumatic stress disorder (PTSD), other types are caused by occupational challenges. The complexity of mental health conditions means that several elements, rather than a single factor, may culminate in physical and/or mental signs and symptoms. This can include long-term sickness, increased absences, poor performance, and constant tiredness or low energy levels (Gray, 1999; Gabriel and Liimatainen, 2000). For early childhood professionals, ever increasing demands and expectations produced at national and local policy level can potentially lead to changes in their own health and wellbeing. Inspection procedures, meeting targets and pressure from leaders have been identified as the most common cause of mental health problems amongst teachers and lecturers (ATL, 2014). Stresses experienced by practitioners working with younger children are also affected by heavy workloads, but there are additional issues here, for example feelings of helplessness when young children are in pain or distress. Overly high expectations are also a risk, as practitioners strive to work above and beyond their roles and responsibilities (Clifford-Poston, 2002). For those working with babies and toddlers, emotional stability is crucial to support practitioners in developing good relationships (Goouch & Powell, 2013).

However, with stigma still surrounding the topic of mental health, two-thirds of employees working in the education sector would not disclose their condition to their employers (ATL, 2014). Negative perceptions towards individuals with conditions such as depression are evident in a study by the NMHDU (2010), which revealed that, based on their findings, over half of the UK public would not offer a person a job if they disclosed a mental health condition. They believed that such a person would be unreliable, more likely to be off sick, and would not work as well or be accepted by other staff.

As an early childhood leader, the care and wellbeing of staff as well as children and families are imperative, as untreated mental health conditions can have a detrimental impact on a member of staff's capacity to work effectively and lead to increased incidences of sick leave and absenteeism. In Sarah-Jane's case, as a Deputy Room Leader, she uses a mix of observational, interpersonal and reflective skills to identify and address potential staff issues at the earliest stage, before they develop into more complex problems. During her interview, she said:

> 'I can talk about how they're feeling if I ever notice they have been particularly quiet or something in the day, I'll go up to them at the end of the day and ask if everything is okay, even if I know they've perhaps just been having a quiet day. I don't want to be ignoring something that could potentially be an underlying issue, like whether they are unhappy with another member of staff, or if that is ever the case, I'd go up to the room leader and then we'll discuss how to deal with it together, if anything is to be taken further we will deal with it as appropriate … I step back and look at what the actual situation is, whether it is good or bad, whether it is staff related. What is it that's causing this? Is it a snide remark? Maybe they're just feeling grumpy today and just taking it out on the nearest person to them. What's going on?

If I've got concerns, I will try and speak to the staff member about it and ask them what's going on, especially if it isn't like them. Half the time, it is nothing. It could be hormonal and they're just taking it out on everyone or it's an issue at home. The key to dealing with things is knowing what the situation is and being able to sit back and be able to reflect on it'.

ACTIVITY 5.2

Re-read the statement provided by Sarah-Jane and consider what you currently have in place or would put in place to support the emotional, social and mental wellbeing of early childhood staff.

➜   Would there need to be different provision or support for those who are students or volunteers within the setting?

Sarah-Jane's response correlates with some of the guidance provided by the National Institute for Health and Care Excellence (NICE, 2015), which recommends that line managers, namely room leaders or other senior staff in early childhood settings, adopt a positive leadership style. Their guidance contains a range of approaches including:

➜   acting as a coach or mentor;
➜   offering each employee help and encouragement to build supportive relationships;
➜   promoting employee engagement and communication;
➜   recognising and praising good performance;
➜   becoming trusted and respected role models.

As discussed earlier in this chapter, mentoring and coaching play a significant role in ensuring that staff can work to the best of their ability within a supportive and encouraging environment. The use of appraisal and supervision meetings provides leaders and their colleagues with an opportunity to reflect on and identify the triggers and causes that may be detrimental to individual health and wellbeing (Sterling Honig, 2010). The findings from these meetings should support the development of appropriate goals and actions, which may include changes to patterns of work, delegating roles, responsibilities and workloads, and ensuring that staff are able to take their breaks and annual leave. On a final note, we are mindful that in some cases there may be underlying health conditions which require the intervention of other professionals. In these cases, it is particularly necessary for leaders to be aware of other mental health-related conditions and recognise the impact that these can have on a practitioner and their wellbeing. Ideally, staff will be open about any challenging physical, emotional or mental health conditions they face. They are more likely to be open if they believe they will be treated fairly and positively, with discussions taking place about best practice for both the member of staff and the setting. If the member of staff feels valued, they are more likely to be supportive of changes which may be needed to adjust their work. As indicated in Chapter 6, this will enable them to be a positive force, engaged in planning changes to ensure the environment is a safe and effective one, for both the member of staff and the team, the children and the families.

SUMMARY AND CONCLUSIONS

This chapter has considered two types of professionals: those who are novices to the sector and develop their own expertise through a voluntary or training route, and those who are established professionals looking to further their knowledge and expertise. Regardless of where practitioners are in terms of their career they all have much to offer, and with the sector becoming increasingly diverse and working with children becoming more attractive, due to opportunities to study higher level qualifications, it is important that early childhood leaders are equipped with the skills to support, facilitate and guide their colleagues. We have also taken into account the challenges that working in the sector presents, particularly in relation to mental health, which has become the focus of recent reports across the early years and education sectors. Leaders must therefore be aware of factors that may impact on their colleagues' ability to work effectively with children and families, and consider how their own skills and expertise can be utilised to address issues at the earliest stage. In Chapter 6 we shall be looking beyond the confines of the leader's setting and considering how leadership is applied across various settings.

RECOMMENDED FURTHER READING

We recommend that you read this very practical article about mentoring:

Chu, M. (2012) 'Observe, reflect and apply: ways to successfully mentor early childhood educators', *Dimensions of Early Childhood*, 40 (3): 20–8. Available at: http://www.southernearlychildhood.org/upload/pdf/Dimensions_Vol40_3_Chu.pdf

6

LEADING DEVELOPMENTS ACROSS A SETTING OR SETTINGS

CHAPTER OBJECTIVES

→ Describe the use of distributed leadership within and across early childhood settings.
→ Consider one's own development as a leader.
→ Discuss ways to develop a culture of leadership.
→ Consider theories of leading change within and across settings.

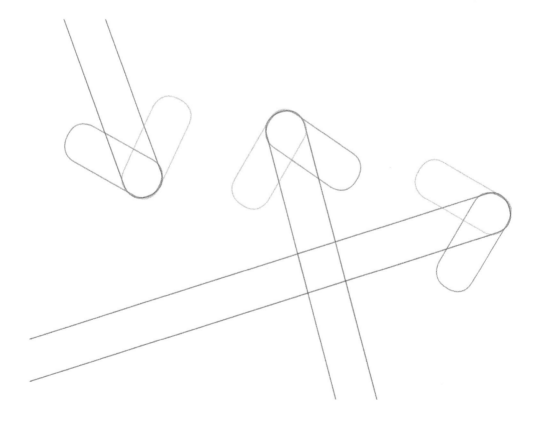

INTRODUCTION

In Chapter 1 we identified that leadership can be enacted in different ways and by different practitioners within the setting. In this chapter, our focus is on leadership enacted by the person who is identified as the overall leader of the setting or setting. In the UK this person may be the setting owner, an appointed manager, a practice leader, or a teacher. A variety of titles are given to this role across different settings. While most of this book is about leading practice, within this chapter we also consider aspects of organisational leadership. This is important in identifying and enacting values for a setting, setting a vision and setting goals which are consistent with the organisational aims, and in ensuring the legal and moral responsibilities of the organisation are met. We consider ways in which to enhance collaborative leadership while retaining authority and responsibility within and across settings. The importance of engaging staff in the development of a work culture, and demonstrating the values of the organisation, is elaborated in this chapter through a focus on the use of communication and collaborative work processes. As Morgan (2006: 137) puts it, we consider how the leader of the setting can go about the 'enactment of a shared reality'.

The early childhood leader must engage with management practice to ensure that provision is of a high standard. Leadership and management may be seen as separate, rather than complementary components, particularly in settings where there is a specific management hierarchy. It is necessary to recognise that across the sector managers require good leadership skills to motivate, empower and develop staff and trainees. As well as concentrating on the identification and enactment of vision and values within a setting, the setting leader will need to ensure that mechanisms are in place to make certain that legal and moral responsibilities are met. Male and Nicholson (2016) distinguish the legal imperative from the moral imperative of ensuring the setting also meets the requirements embedded in the expectations of the local community.

These responsibilities include ensuring that:

→ staff are appropriately qualified;
→ there is a suitable mechanism for staff development;
→ staff are supported to be reflective and reflexive and to develop their knowledge, understanding and skills to enact their role effectively;
→ legal responsibilities are met, for example regarding staff ratios, safeguarding, inclusion, equality, data protection;
→ appropriate records are kept and shared responsibly.

The key traits of a strong leader, which we referred to in Chapter 1, include intelligence, using initiative, and the ability to persuade others (Eagly & Carli, 2007). Within an early childhood setting, with a largely female workforce, a participatory, democratic leadership style is preferred (Scrivens, 2002).

DISTRIBUTED LEADERSHIP

In Chapter 1 we identified that early childhood settings might make use of distributed leadership as a way of achieving democratic leadership. In this sense, leadership is embedded into a variety of roles within the setting and therefore there is an expectation on practitioners to influence best practice. The way in which this distributed or shared leadership operates effectively is through engaging with a culture and the sharing of learning and knowledge within a setting. Aubrey et al. (2012) and Heikka and Waniganayake (2011) propose that distributed leadership is embedded within the way that relationships are built and the way that staff are supported to develop confidence, and hence be able to undertake leadership within their role. In this way, leadership is enabled across the range of practitioners within the setting. Aubrey et al. (2012) also identify from their case study research that distributed leadership is not exclusive to situations where the team is face to face, but can also be effective across settings. For example, where an organisation has several different settings the strong relationships across and between settings can enable sharing of good practice.

Enacting distributed leadership assumes effective communication within and between settings, with a focus on the development of strong working relationships, alongside a culture where every member of the team is trusted by its other members. Using a distributed approach to leadership recognises that leadership can sit within a number of roles and different stakeholders can be effective leaders of practice. Rah (2013) describes the way in which leadership was distributed within a school community in the USA to meet a particular need. The sudden arrival of a large number of Thai children in one school was led through a 'FAST (families and schools together)' (2013: 63) programme. This process relied on the involvement of teachers, parents and a range of other professional groups, and aimed to enable integration and set the scene for the children to be able to access the academic curriculum. The eight-week programme was funded, enabling the use of facilitators to involve and work with the families and other professionals. Rah (2013) describes the collaboration, collective effort and co-ordination which formed part of the programme, and identifies this with the components of distributed leadership.

REFLECTION POINT

To what extent are aspects of leadership 'distributed' within the team with which you work? How would this leadership style compare to settings which may adopt a more authoritative or laissez-faire approach?

Bennett et al. (2003) and Heikka et al. (2012) provide useful summaries and an analysis of the research into distributed leadership and its use within the early childhood sector. In our view distributed leadership fits well with the values of early childhood sector, recognising the roles of all practitioners in leading and influencing good practice.

In some cases, early childhood leaders may oversee the provision of more than one setting, which form part of a group, chain or cluster. Providers may be based across numerous sites regionally, nationally or internationally, with leaders undertaking the role of an Area or Regional Manager. Their role is to work with managers of individual branches to capture and disseminate best practice and monitor the quality of provision (DCSF, 2008a). Local Authorities have also offered individual settings support through the use of Early Years Consultants/Advisors, who act as catalysts for quality improvement and provide guidance on wider issues such as training, funding and resources (NDNA, 2015). This is achieved through a combination of observation, modelling, coaching and having the confidence to challenge practice, as a means of making it more effective (DCSF, 2010). There are potential undesirable implications for undertaking such roles, notably having to work with a greater number of settings across wider geographical locations. The demand for services may potentially affect the frequency and continuity of support provided, hence consultants and advisers need strong organisational skills and the ability to communicate and negotiate deadlines and meetings with each setting (Education and Training Inspectorate, 2014).

Furthermore, since the publication of *More Great Childcare*, Ofsted have been made the sole arbiter of quality in response to claims that Local Authorities were needlessly duplicating inspections (DfE, 2013). In response, there was concern that local knowledge and expertise would be lost, with some Local Authorities arguing that their role was not to inspect but to address the need to improve quality, adding that both services should complement the role of the other (4Children, 2013; Gaunt & Morton, 2013).

Not all leaders associated with groups of settings work independently. In recent years changes across the sector, combined with annual funding cuts, have led to children's centres merging and forming clusters, comprising of two or more settings which work collaboratively in a formal or informal manner. Groups of managers share good practice and distribute knowledge and expertise, with the aim of raising standards across several sites. This approach to leadership is becoming more widespread, with a growing number of centres moving towards a more distributed form of service provision and formulating strategic goals in partnership with other sites (Sharp et al., 2012; Sylva et al., 2015). The sharing of good practice was deemed greatly beneficial by our interviewees, with many embracing the opportunity to learn from other professionals working in different settings and roles across the sector. As leaders it is important to remember that the early childhood sector is constantly evolving and changing, hence the injection of new and inspirational ideas plays a pivotal role in providing new ways of working that can be adapted to the needs and vision of a setting.

DEVELOPING ONESELF AS THE LEADER OF A SETTING

As a leader of a setting or settings, it is easy to get so involved in developing others that you might ignore your own needs. It is important to consider yourself and your own development needs, and this section identifies some of the ways you can do this. For your own development as a leader you will need to feel confident to undertake your role, sufficiently knowledgeable about the current issues in early childhood education and care, and able to seek appropriate support or advice from others. You will also need to reflect on your role and abilities, and plan to develop as your role develops and changes.

REFLECTION POINT

Considering your own role in a setting or within your workplace, how do you ensure that your skills, knowledge and experience are kept up to date? Where do you access support or guidance to inform your own professional development needs?

Keeping up to date is highly necessary. You will need to know about current government and local authority policies and procedures, developments in early childhood education and care practice, and the latest research to support effective practice. Think about what you currently do to keep up to date.

You might have thought about your local or wider network of colleagues within the sector, publications you read regularly, circulars you receive, courses you attend, or professional groups you belong to. Developing a network for your own support and development can be a very useful way of keeping up to date and developing new ideas. For example, when you attend a training course, do you share ideas with others, do you take note of their contact details and have some way of starting discussions with them? Some practitioners start social networking sites to share ideas and as a forum for asking for advice, others arrange monthly get-togethers to discuss issues. Professional groups such as TACTYC (tactyc.org.uk) and PACEY (www.pacey.org.uk) offer networking opportunities at a national level, and disseminate news and research for the benefit of the early childhood workforce. Such organisations can be particularly helpful in seeing the bigger picture of the world of early childhood education and care. Such groups also produce professional literature to enable the workforce to keep up to date with policy and practice. Current research and activities to develop effective practice are also shared within early childhood research conferences, for example those run by the British Early Childhood Education Research Association (BECERA) and the European Early Childhood Education Research Association (EECERA). There are plenty of other organisations across the UK and the world, and your choice will depend on your aims and aspirations. Becoming a member of such organisations gives you access to a network of like-minded research active practitioners.

The extent to which you become actively involved in such organisations will be up to you and your identified development needs. Chapter 9 in this book considers reflection as a professional attribute and a component of leadership. Reflection can be a very useful way to identify your own development needs from which you can discuss those needs with your own line manager and seek out sources to support their development. Another way in which to support your development is by setting goals within your appraisal. In Chapter 5 we considered how the role of feedback supports professional development and allows leaders to review their current practice. Perhaps a more challenging route to your own development and the development of the setting is to actively seek feedback. This feedback could be from the children, from other staff, from the families, or from the wider interprofessional team. Feedback is sometimes provided spontaneously, in the form of compliments or complaints. It is also often sought informally in the form of conversations with others about 'how things are going'. For leaders working with more than one setting, the role of purposeful feedback must not be underestimated. It requires a two-way channel of communication, in which the leader and recipient evaluate, reflect and identify the next steps for improvement (DCSF, 2010). Having a formal mechanism to receive feedback can also be a useful tool in the development of practice, for example meetings with families, family forums, and opportunities for children to have their voices heard about the running of the setting. Ofsted, through their inspections of provision, provide feedback in terms of the quality of the education provided within the setting and the extent to which this meets the EYFS standards. This feedback also includes a judgement about the leadership within the setting, which can be used for reflection on one's own development.

DEVELOPING OTHERS WITHIN THE SETTING

A large part of this book is about how to take on leadership within a variety of roles. Thus, the book is useful for the leader of a setting or settings in supporting workforce development. For example, in Chapter 3 we discuss the room leader's role and opportunity for development, and in Chapter 4 we discuss the role of the key person. Equally we have incorporated a great deal about developing staff into Chapter 5 where we discuss mentorship, coaching, the use of supervision and the use of performance review. Part of the leader's role is to encourage an environment where staff want to develop. A setting which recognises and celebrates the strengths amongst team members, and supports staff development, demonstrates that it values its people. A key part of staff development is supporting them in developing their ability to be reflective and reflexive (see Chapter 9), to value the child and their family, and to have a vision for their practice (Whalley, 2011b). Within this staff will need support to develop their knowledge and understanding of children and their development, learning, and families and communities.

DEVELOPING AN ORGANISATIONAL CULTURE OF LEADERSHIP

As a leader of a setting or settings, you have the potential to develop leadership as a *culture* (Daft, 2011). To do this, you will need to put in place structures, policies, procedures and ways of working which support such a culture. These initiatives will be derived from the values of the setting. As a collaborative leader, these values will have originated not just from your own views, but also from those of the staff and families involved in the setting. The culture of leadership is derived from the relationships you have with the children and families, the staff in the setting, and the other members of the multiprofessional team with whom you have contact. Establishing and maintaining strong communication and positive interaction with others is vital for developing this culture of leadership. As a leader you recognise that situations are not static and unchanging, but rather that society, policy and communities do change and thus the setting will need to be adaptive to these changes. In a setting with a leadership culture, your interactions with and involvement of all stakeholders will enable you to support group decision making and maintain a socially relevant organisation.

Choices will have to be made about whether to make specific appointments for specific leadership roles. The challenge here is to avoid moving down a technical-rational route for the organisational structure, and instead enact roles which will function to empower staff and enhance the ability of the workforce. In other words, the choices made about the structure of the setting will evidence your values and impact on the culture within the setting. Research clearly demonstrates the value of roles such as the 'Early Years Professional' or 'Head of Early Years Practice' (Hadfield et al., 2012; Davis & Capes, 2013; Davis & Ryder, 2015) which have led to positive changes in practice. Organisations that appoint leaders of early years practice evidence positive developments of practice with benefits for children and families. While these roles have a specific leadership remit (early childhood practice), the roles are not task focused. Rather they embrace the complexity of early childhood practice and use democratic methods to enhance practice, thereby improving outcomes for children and families.

Within larger organisations, such as nursery chains, it is easy for the management structure to become very hierarchical, with limited practitioner representation in decisions taken for the organisation. Effective organisations recognise the importance of practitioners' voices, as they are in daily contact with children and families, and therefore will enable these to be heard so that this expertise can be integrated into the decision-making process. A flatter management structure, with distributed leadership, enables this.

An effective structure was employed by a provider which currently operates four settings in different parts of England. We explored this structure as part of the research for this book. Each of the settings has a Head of Early Years Practice, as well as a Head who leads on the resourcing of the setting. Within each team are senior early years educators, early years educators, practitioners working towards level three, and apprentices. The majority of staff take key person roles and engage with families to ensure best outcomes. The Head of Early Years Practice within each setting is responsible for the quality of care and education within that setting, but also operates strategically across settings to share good practice and develop new ways of working, for example in response to policy changes.

ACTIVITY 6.1: THE STRUCTURE OF THE SETTING(S)

Map out the management structure of your setting or settings. Think about the roles rather than the persons in those roles. To what extent does the structure support your values and those of the practitioners and families within the setting?

Activity 6.1 is not necessarily very easy. It requires you to be very familiar with your own values and the values in the setting. It may require you to take some time to reflect about the structure and how effective it is. There may be elements of the structure which work well, but others which do not. For example, to what extent is leadership of early childhood *practice* supported by the organisational structure within the setting?

Leadership of practice has been identified as very important for a positive impact on outcomes for children (Hadfield et al., 2012). Colmer (2009) refers to the need to embed this culture of leading practice within each setting in order to achieve a high quality setting. She argues that a culture of learning must be embedded within the organisation to realise this high quality of practice, and describes how to do this effectively through the use of 'reflective practice and action learning' (2009: 108). The leader is encouraged to develop a culture where all employees engage with their own development. In our research, we saw this in evidence through the way each member of staff was encouraged to reflect both formally and informally and to learn from their reflections. We also saw staff involved in regular development meetings with their line manager, to consider their own development and the needs of the setting. Valuing staff, by encouraging their development, provided a sense of being trusted to the practitioners in our study (Davis & Ryder, 2015).

The emphasis within a setting will be primarily to provide an effective setting which enables children's holistic development. The leader must regularly engage in reflecting on the culture of the setting, and how the values espoused by that setting are evidenced in practice. Learning from this reflection will enable the leader to make changes to practice which will enhance the quality of the setting.

So far within this chapter we have considered how to develop yourself and others as leaders and how to enact leadership within and across settings. At times, organisations will need to make significant changes to their current practice. In the next section, we explore ways in which to enact major change within and across settings.

ENACTING MAJOR CHANGE WITHIN OR ACROSS SETTINGS

Within the field of early childhood policy regularly changes, and this often requires settings to make significant changes to their ways of working. In England, for example, the introduction of the new and then revised Early Years Foundation Stage (DfE, 2014a; 2014b) as a curriculum for the education of young children required local policy and procedures to be introduced within settings to ensure legal compliance with the new national policy requirements. In circumstances such as these, transformational leadership is required by the setting leader (Burns, 1978; Northouse, 2015).

To be a transformative leader, you will firstly need to be informed yourself about the new policy. Leaders become informed by attending training events, discussing the new policy with their network of early childhood colleagues, and reading the professional press. Local authorities or other government bodies typically issue guidance, which is often fairly broad and requires interpretation within the local context of the setting. There may be local authority advisers to offer support in understanding the new policy. From your understanding of the required changes, you will then need to develop a new and clear vision for the setting. This must include a vision of how the setting will differ once the change has occurred.

Many stakeholders will begrudge policy change, particularly if the present system appears to be working well. You will need to be prepared to deal with resentment against and negative views of the need to change. To do this, you will need to prepare ways to engage with all stakeholders both cognitively and emotionally (Northouse, 2015). In other words, it is your responsibility to clearly communicate to all stakeholders why the change is needed, so they are then able to understand why you are initiating that change. It is also your responsibility to support the stakeholder to move to a point where they will support you in wanting the change.

We are emphasising here your responsibility as the leader of a setting in instigating major change. As a collaborative leader you will do this through shared leadership rather than alone. Using a model for planning change, such as those provided by Lewin (Burnes, 2004) or Kotter (1996), can be very supportive for the setting leader.

In Chapter 1 we referred to the importance of motivation. Understanding of the factors which affect a practitioner's motivation is necessary for strong leadership across and within settings. A leader will be keen to create the positive environment which is generated from motivated staff. Encouraging motivation can include setting realistic targets which will enable the practitioner to be involved and demonstrate their abilities (Locke, 1968). It is also important for a leader to be fair and equitable, and ensure favouritism is not shown (Adams, 1965).

Work by Davis (2012) indicates that the early childhood leader intelligently selects relevant theoretical concepts to support them in considering the best ways in which to enact leadership and change within their setting. Early childhood leaders are able to be selective and choose from a range of theoretical concepts. We consider some of these theoretical approaches below, and link them to the work of the early childhood leader. You might want to refer back to your reflection in Chapter 1, about linking theory to practice.

CHANGE THEORY

We live in a society where changes are occurring at a very rapid rate as technology develops and international communications increase. We also have to respond to changes in international and national policy, implementing new ways of working within settings. Managing planned change is now a vital skill for those in leadership positions, and much of the literature about change is about planned change. We recognise, however, that some changes can be unplanned and unpredictable, or occur with very short notice. In these cases experience of planning change can be invaluable, enabling you to draw on communication skills and a collaborative culture in order to go through periods of change and emerge positively on the other side.

There are a number of steps in the change process, described differently by different authors, and we have included references to some of these in the chapter. Essentially effective leadership and management of change requires a problem-solving approach with open communication with all those involved. Change needs to be balanced with continuity – too much change leads to fatigue. There is a need to recognise that although planned change aims to improve it will bring losses, and is likely to be perceived by some, at least initially, as detrimental.

Many people want immediate results from change, yet these results may not be apparent for many months or years, and keeping going with the change can demand tenacity. Effective communication throughout the change process is essential for positive outcomes. Change can have unintended and unwanted outcomes as well as desirable ones. Keeping in mind the original reason for the change is important, as a way of judging its effectiveness. As a leader of change, try to take a long-term and strategic view. Think about how many changes are occurring at the same time and about whether there will be time for the change to take effect: you many need to think about the different levels of change (for example, regional, national, international) and therefore will have to consider the differing values, ideals and cultures at each of these levels.

PLANNED CHANGE

Kurt Lewin (a social scientist who worked to resolve social conflict) first coined the term 'planned change' to distinguish this from the unintended or accidental changes which may happen to an organisation (Burnes, 2004). Lewin's theory stresses the balance between forces which drive the change forward and forces which hold the change back. Lewin recommends undertaking a *force field analysis* before making a change, to determine which forces are at work to support the planned change, but also which forces are likely to be opposing or inhibiting the change. These positive and negative forces might include people, systems, procedures and policy. Lewin calls these 'driving forces' and 'restraining forces'. Mapping the forces, with arrows of different sizes working for and against the change, can give a visual picture from which to analyse the factors which might influence the change, and by doing so will take account of these in the plan for change. For example, a change in national policy will be a strong driving force for change, whereas a member of staff who does not want to change the status quo can act as a restraining force.

Lewin suggested a three-stage process for making a change. The first stage, unfreezing, requires the leader to generate a feeling for the need for change, clearly stating the desired outcome of that change. At this stage a democratic leader will involve all the stakeholders in finding ways to change and in selecting the best way to undertake the change. The leader of the change will make best use of the driving forces and motivate the stakeholders to want to change.

The second stage of Lewin's model of planned change is the moving stage. At this point communication is crucial so that everyone can see why there is a need for change. Plans are made and staff are involved in commenting on and trying out the new way of working. Detailed further plans will be made. Positive messages about how well the change is going are often used during this stage.

The third and final stage, refreezing, reinforces the change and the new working patterns, policies or procedures are put in place. During this stage the leader needs to ensure that the values implicit in the new change become embedded. Effective communication skills will be needed.

Lewin's work on planned change influenced many other theorists, for example, Reddin, Havelock, and Rogers (Barr & Dowding, 2015). Kotter's (1996) model of planned change is likely to be familiar to many who work in early childhood settings. This is an eight-stage model, which includes a need to:

→   establish a sense of urgency – to help people realise that change is needed;
→   establish a team that is able to guide the change – this gets people involved and helps to take account of different views;
→   develop a vision and strategy – to clearly set out what things will look like once the change is in place;
→   communicate the vision widely – everyone involved needs to know, and typically there needs to be several opportunities for people to hear about and discuss the change;
→   empower staff to act to achieve the vision – giving people different responsibilities to support the change to happen will enable them to become more committed to the change;
→   set short-term achievable goals – particularly if the change is over a period of time, having stepped changes, where each step can be achieved at a time, can support forward movement of the change;
→   keep the sense of urgency – don't assume that the change will happen on its own, it needs to be kept in people's awareness, and also needs to continue to be led;
→   make the changes last/endure – don't abandon the change once it has happened, put in place ways to support its ongoing success.

If you have to plan change, we hope you will make use of some of this change theory to support you to effectively lead change. We have included scenarios throughout this book, based on real early childhood leadership practice, exploring how early childhood practitioners have led change in their own settings.

ACTIVITY 6.2: THINKING ABOUT A
THEORY OF CHANGE

For this activity, we want you to think about a change which you have led, or perhaps a change which you are about to lead or want to lead. Take time to consider the use of Lewin's model of planned change, or Kotter's model, and think through the different elements of the change. You might find it helpful to map this out on a large piece of paper.

Trying out the use of a model in this way is a helpful way of thinking more deeply about the purpose of the change and how exactly it will be enacted. It is also necessary to think about how this change will be maintained, rather than practise reverting to its original form. If you are keen to read more about how practitioners use theory to enact change, Davis (2012) explores this more thoroughly.

RESISTANCE TO CHANGE

Many of us enjoy working within a structure and routines which have become comfortable and familiar. Change will alter this and introduce unfamiliar and often unknown quantities. Children, families and staff will want to know how the change will affect them individually as well as the nature of the change for the organisation. An effective leader will be open and willing to discuss change, but must also identify those who are resistant and be pro-active in dealing with that resistance.

Reactions to change can range from negative to positive, from sabotage to overt resistance, passive resistance, denial, avoidance, blame, moaning and groaning, confronting the issues, problem solving, and planning to make the change happen (Daft, 2011). Individual resistance may become apparent through fear of the unknown or comfort in the known, and this fear can make it difficult for people to take on board all that is being communicated. Some staff may also not value the need for change, particularly in cases where a leader has a specific long-term vision. In Valarie's case, her own professional development opened her up to new pedagogical approaches to learning, which she felt would greatly benefit the children and families attending the setting. During her interview, she conveyed that despite her enthusiasm and passion, her team appeared uninterested in adapting to a new means of working, which led to changes being gradually implemented over a much longer time frame. It is the role of the leader to support individuals to identify and cope with the way change is affecting them. Working collaboratively with all those involved in the change, and communicating honestly and clearly, are important, as is a focus on the benefits of the change.

The person driving the change needs to have a number of skills as a 'change agent' (Daft, 2011). This leader needs to be able to listen to others and take varied suggestions, making a workable structure out of them. They need to be able to motivate others and communicate effectively and regularly. The change agent needs to be based in reality and set achievable targets, but also needs to be able to communicate the vision for change confidently. It goes without saying that a leader who is respected and trusted by staff and families will be able to more successfully lead change.

There will inevitably be some people who will resist change, and the ability to manage this resistance is a skill required by the leader. To lead a major change in a setting, an effective change agent needs to have sufficient authority – either through their position or their personality. They also need to be in a position to consult with others and make well informed and balanced judgements.

SUMMARY AND CONCLUSIONS

We started this chapter with a consideration of distributed leadership, a way of leading which can be empowering for the workforce by recognising and developing leadership within the wider team. We have also considered ways in which the leader can think about their own development, with opportunities for networking locally, nationally and internationally. The importance of the culture of the setting has been emphasised, and the leader's role in developing that culture and setting clear values within the setting has been described. The latter part of the chapter has considered how to lead change, and we have provided examples of models of leading planned change that can be a practical tool for leaders. Not everyone wants to change, so the consideration of resistance to change has been included in order that this can also be considered when change is planned.

RECOMMENDED FURTHER READING

You might find this Department of Education publication useful reading:

Education and Training Inspectorate (2014) *An Evaluation of the Role of the Early Years Specialist*. Bangor: Department of Education. Available at www.etini.gov.uk/index/ surveys-evaluations/surveys-evaluations-pre-school-centre-and-nursery-school/surveys- evaluations-pre-school-2014/an-evaluation-of-the-role-of-the-early-years-specialist.pdf

7

WORKING WITH FAMILIES

CHAPTER OBJECTIVES

→ Discuss the importance of working in partnership with families.
→ Consider whether the setting is accessible to families.
→ Describe the development of professional relationships with families with a range of needs.
→ Identify the need to protect early childhood staff.

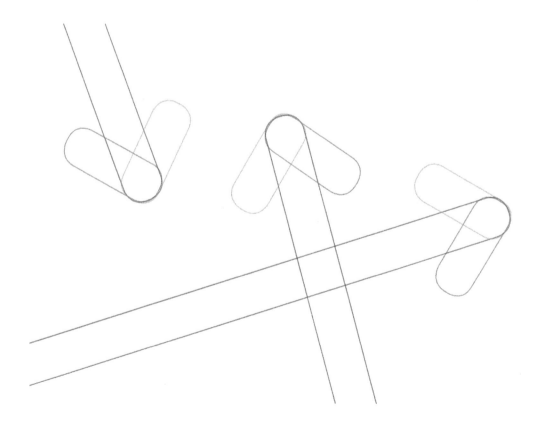

INTRODUCTION

This chapter explores how relationships between practitioners and families can be developed and sustained, to ensure that each child receives the best possible care and education at the start of their life. We cover the importance of communication and reflection in ensuring that settings are accessible and the diverse needs of families are recognised. Furthermore, we consider some of the challenges that families face, relating to mental health, disabilities, family breakdown and transitions. We believe that in this day and age, early childhood leaders are faced with managing and supporting a growing number of issues that impact on both the child and the family as a whole. While early childhood practitioners are not trained to be counsellors, social workers or health professionals, it is essential that they not only recognise when families are in need, but are also able to safeguard themselves. We shall therefore explore how early childhood staff can stay safe and professional when dealing with difficult relationships and complex situations.

In recent decades, family structures have become more diverse and complex, and in combination with socio-economic and political changes, increased pressures and responsibilities there has been an increased focus to support families in need (DfES, 2003). The terms 'parents as partners' and 'working in partnership with parents and carers' suggest a conjoined effort to provide young children with the best possible start in life. We argue that these terms are somewhat limiting, considering that grandparents, older siblings, other relatives and foster parents play a valuable role in a child's life, particularly in cases where a parent is unable to care or provide for their child. Therefore, throughout this chapter, the term 'families' has been used to encompass and embrace the various environments and family structures children are raised in.

Since the introduction of *Every Child Matters* in 2003 (DfES, 2003), greater emphasis has been placed on the pivotal role parents and carers have in supporting their child's learning and development. As prime educators they support early socialisation and set the foundations for mental and emotional development. However, their views and understanding on education and learning differ from those held by people working directly with young children (Kelley-Laine, 1988; Harris & Goodall, 2007). Parents may not necessarily recognise the knowledge, expertise and influence they possess in relating to their role as an educator (Atkin et al., 1988; DfES, 2007). Leaders therefore play a key role in empowering, encouraging and supporting families, while at the same time consulting with parents and carers and sharing information regarding their child's progress (DfE, 2014b).

RECOGNISING THE IMPORTANCE OF PARTNERSHIPS WITH FAMILIES

Historically, the relationship between families and settings has, at times, been turbulent. Schools in particular were reported to be unwelcoming, inaccessible, and hostile environments for parents and carers. Some studies report that parents were often dissuaded from speaking directly to teachers or were not permitted to enter the premises. Furthermore, there were instances where there was a lack of information, communication and consultation regarding their child's progress (Green, 1968; Wolfendale, 1992). In response, schools argued that parental attitudes and approaches to raising their children made it challenging for them to do their job properly (Hughes et al., 1994). Hence, instead of educational settings and home environments being viewed as complementary learning establishments, they were perceived to be separate and almost incompatible entities. These issues are not restricted to the maintained sector, as private and voluntary settings have also reported challenges relating to engaging with families. A report by Royston and Rodrigues (2013) conveyed that some families felt unwelcome or under-confident using children's centre services, which had implications for them seeking and receiving support. Interviewees from our study added that there were occasions when parents did not listen to or act upon the advice and recommendations provided by the early childhood practitioners. While they acknowledged that parents have the final say in their child's learning and development, they expressed frustration at some parents not understanding their role or level of pedagogical knowledge and training.

Despite these issues, the early childhood sector has generally been supportive and inclusive towards parents. In the 1960s a shortage of nursery provision led to the Playgroup Movement, with mothers setting up their own early childhood services. Parents were therefore at the very heart of provision, leading to an expansion of services nationally (Tizard et al., 1976; Cohen & Fraser, 1991). Changes to policies and procedures have also played a significant role over the past 40 years, addressing a number of the issues discussed earlier. The publication of the Plowden Report in 1967 made reference to 'participation by parents', a phrase that set out to encourage parents into schools, recommending numerous strategies to establish stronger links with the home (CACE, 1967). Throughout the 1970s there was a significant increase in parental involvement, through parent-teacher consultations, reading schemes and parent helper schemes. Since the Plowden Report parental involvement has predominantly been accepted as a component of professional good practice, with the launch of the Early Years Foundation Stage (EYFS) placing a greater emphasis on settings and families working in a coherent and consistent manner (Vincent, 1996; DCSF, 2008c).

Developing effective partnerships was viewed as a means for parents and practitioners to work together to seek the best outcome for each child (DCSF, 2007; 2008b). The term 'partnership' is often associated with the relationship between parents and early childhood professionals. An emphasis on equal or coordinated partnerships suggests that there is a shared level of expertise between parents and practitioners. The parents are experts on their child, while the practitioner is an expert in the care and education of children within the context of an individual or group setting (Kernan, 2012). However, Boag-Munro (2014) argues that the term 'partnership' is poorly defined, as it implies a relationship centred around power and effort. In contrast, terms such as 'involvement' and 'participation' suggest a working relationship based on a contribution and collaboration by both parties. Despite these different views, it is important for leaders to recognise the essential role families play, particularly in relation to their engagement with the setting. Practitioners themselves may have their own terms and definitions to describe the relationship they have with families, but the emphasis remains on both parties working closely together to support the learning and development of the children in their care.

Partnerships are not restricted to parents, but may entail working with grand-parents, older siblings, extended family members and foster carers. For children looked after by kin carers, namely older siblings, neighbours, friends of the fam-ily, a common problem relates to underachievement at school and the increased possibility of behavioural or emotional challenges (Farmer & Moyers, 2008; Hunt et al., 2008). In Chapter 4 we discussed the role of attachment and the key person, drawing attention to feelings of anxiety and abandonment that may be experienced by the child. In cases where practitioners are working with young children who are looked after by other adults, there may have been numerous transitions experienced by a child in a short space of time. They may demonstrate behaviours that can be misinterpreted and need additional support in building secure attachments, not just in the setting but also with the adults responsible for their care and wellbeing (Frame et al., 2004). The following example from a private day nursery, taking part in our study, highlights how practitioners work with these families:

> In addition to families from mixed socio-economic backgrounds, Colette and her early childhood team have supported foster families and families going through the adoption process. The experiences of these families vary, with some children attending nursery for the short term, others settling quickly into the nursery environment and some experiencing attachment issues, as a result of transitioning from one family set up to the next. Colette adds that attachment and behaviour are areas that require the staff to explore how they can support the child, with strategies such as one-to-one support recognised as being effective in some cases.

From this example, the setting takes into account that the needs of individual chil-dren and their foster families greatly differ; with staff applying their knowledge and understanding of child development and attachment theory to their practice. When working with different family groups, it is important for leaders to consider whether their team has the relevant skills, knowledge and training to support them in their role. If this is not the case then further training and support are needed to equip practitioners with the knowledge, skills and confidence required to work effectively.

HARD-TO-REACH FAMILIES OR HARD-TO-REACH SETTINGS?

As discussed previously in this chapter, developing effective partnerships with fami-lies is a key requirement for practitioners working in early childhood. There are numerous books and articles available that discuss how settings can become more inclusive and accessible to families, and these provide many ideas and initiatives that can be used. However, maintaining these relationships can be a challenge in itself. Barriers relating to material deprivation, family social class and maternal levels of education may impact on families' abilities to fully engage with settings, regardless of the approaches and initiatives that are implemented (Deforges & Abouchaar, 2003). Families who fall into the above categories are often described in literature as 'hard-to-reach', a term that suggests some form of inaccessibility in relation to early childhood care and education services. This is perceived to be a broad expression as there are numerous influential factors, including the character-istics and needs of marginalised groups, the experiences of different agencies and practitioners working with 'hard-to-reach' families and locally defined priorities (Docherty et al., 2004).

Additional terms, such as 'non-responsive' and 'hard-to-engage', have been criticised as potentially stigmatising families, with some settings rejecting these descriptors in favour of 'families in need' or 'disadvantaged families' (Lord et al., 2011). Organisations participating in a study by Cortis et al. (2009) expressed their reluctance to use labels, as they felt these detracted from the notion of client engage-ment being the responsibility of the services and not the individual. Participants in our study focused more on the needs of individual families rather than using labels, recognising those who needed additional support and having the confidence to seek referrals or ask for support from other colleagues when required.

ACTIVITY 7.1

Which of the following statements do you feel best describes the prime challenge of engaging with families?

→   The families are hard-to-reach.
→   The settings are hard-to-reach.

What is the rationale behind your views? Consider whether the setting is accessible and inclusive to the diverse needs families present. Which groups of families within your local area are not accessing early childhood services? What might be the reason behind this?

For leaders working in the early childhood sector, they may question who the aforementioned groups and individuals are and what would class them as being 'hard-to-reach'. A study by Boag-Munro and Evangelou (2012) acknowledged that this is a broad area and developed two categories to represent different circum-stances. The first, families in voluntary isolation, was comprised of a diverse range of groups, including sex workers, refugee and asylum seekers, prisoners' families, faith-based groups, and families experiencing some form of addiction. It was noted that these groups may feel fearful or threatened at the thought of working with agencies and professionals, in light of their personal circumstances. The second category centred on families who have reservations about service interventions. Numerous concerns and anxieties were identified relating to leaving the child at a childcare setting, distrusting those in authority, or, in some cases, being unwilling or uninterested in receiving support or cooperating with agencies. Campbell (2011) adds that such groups may demonstrate low levels of engagement, exhibit high levels of inertia in relation to overcoming perceived barriers to participation, or fail to attend meetings and respond to communications. For some parents their own experiences with education may lead to suspicion and distrust, which in turn can result in the deterioration of their relationship with practitioners (McConkey, 1985).

From this evidence it would almost appear that much responsibility on engagement lies with the families, particularly in cases where there is an unwillingness to develop and maintain effective partnerships with practitioners and agencies that parents have the right to access for support. A counter-argument pertains to the notion that settings and practitioners themselves may be potential or realised barriers to engagement. Ward (2013) describes such settings as 'hard-to-access', as families are eligible to use their services but may not do so. Studies carried out on Sure Start Children's Centres have provided further insight into the challenges that parents themselves experience. Royston and Rodrigues (2013) discovered that several factors led to families not using their local children's centre, including transport costs or a lack of adequate transport to settings, services being located at different centres that may be hard-to-access, and centre operational hours being incompatible or inflexible for parents or carers with work commitments. Rallings' (2014) findings added that low-level public awareness and a lack of understanding regarding the purpose of children's centres have additionally led to families being unaware of the services provided. Since the economic crisis in 2008 new barriers and challenges have emerged, imposed by local and central government rather than individual settings. Sure Start Children's Centres are increasingly working as multiple sites, grouping with other centres in light of decreased budgets and funding pressures. Furthermore, the trend of centre closures was predicted to continue, with over 100 centres expected to close within the 12 months following the 2014 Sure Start Children's Centres census (4Children, 2014). The impact of this, along with reduced opening times and the reduction or scrapping of specific programmes and services, has meant that some families no longer have access to local providers and that settings are faced with the challenge of being unable to fully meet targets pertaining to local need. While this research relates to children's centre provision, it raises the question as to how accessible, welcoming and engaging all early childhood settings are.

ACTIVITY 7.2

As a practitioner, consider the following questions and how they relate to provision:

→   How welcoming and supportive are we to families using our services?
→   Do we have a good reputation, and if so, how can we send out a message to relay this to potential users?
→   What is it about myself or us that is unique when compared to other settings?
→   How do we make families feel part of our 'community', and what opportunities do we provide to receive their feedback, suggestions and comments?

Over the remainder of the chapter, we shall explore professional relationships with families, how they can be supported in challenging circumstances, and how leaders can safeguard themselves in practice.

PROFESSIONAL RELATIONSHIPS WITH FAMILIES

The early childhood sector has experienced a considerable shift over the past 20 years, with a greater emphasis on professionalism. Partnerships between families and professionals should ideally be active, with the aim to share some of the same goals (Atkin et al., 1988). We say 'ideally' as some families may find it challenging to devote time and energy to building an effective relationship with the setting, in light of career, financial and personal commitments. As discussed in the OPERA section in Chapter 2, parents make a valuable contribution to our knowledge and understanding of their children, and the links between the home environment and the setting play a crucial role in developing relationships with families. Having conversations to explore each family's needs and expectations has evidently been a means of developing suitable learning experiences and educational opportunities for children and families alike:

> 'I'm quite a firm believer that children learn through play. I'm sending him [eldest child] to preschool to integrate with other children without me being there, so he can communicate with other adults as well as he can communicate with myself. I expect from them to give him tools that I can't give him at home, so basically, exploring even more activities … to explore social skills. I expect them to communicate with me as well as I would expect to be communicating with them. For example, if he's not been himself or if I notice anything different in his behaviour, I'll expect them to pick up on things like that too'. (Susan, a Maternity Nurse Trainer, discussing her expectations of preschool staff from a parent perspective)

There are parents who wish to be engaged, but find it difficult to do so. As leaders, it is necessary to explore other means of reaching out and including them. Individuals working in the sector shared a range of approaches to engage with families, including the use of technology, for example emails, websites and online learning journals, and face-to-face meetings, such as parent evenings and informal meetings.

Our interviews with early childhood practitioners and professionals revealed that professional relationships differ greatly depending on roles and responsibilities and the type of provider or service they offer. All participants shared a vision of ensuring that they were meeting the needs of children and families to the best of their abilities. In many cases they would offer advice and support covering numerous topics, including learning, transitions and attachment. For professionals working as nannies and childminders, they were aware of complications that could arise from their close relationships with parents. In many cases, leaders would go above and beyond their duties, washing children's clothes and feeding those they expected were living in poverty, as well as acting as advisers and mentors to parents.

Some of the interviewees reiterated the importance of professional boundaries and acknowledged that the parents would have the final say regarding decision-making procedures. In these cases parents were very much the 'employers' and leaders were provided with high levels of responsibilities, which in the case of nannies could mean they were left to care for the children for several days independently at home or abroad. However, these parents would additionally be reliant on the nanny's support, particularly in cases where their long working hours meant they missed much of their child's day. Garris Christian (2006) recommends that educators recognise different parenting styles and family boundaries, respecting their need for control and avoiding stereotypes. It is important to remember that families will not necessarily share their whole personal history with practitioners, and although over time and with the build-up of trust this may change, there is still a need to respect parents' privacy and wishes, which can be a huge juggling act for those working in the early childhood sector.

SUPPORTING FAMILIES WITH TRANSITIONS

For many families, the move from home to an early childhood setting or from an early childhood setting to school is an emotive experience. Early childhood leaders often come across parents and carers who are distressed and upset at leaving their child at the setting, those who will ring several times a day to check on their child, or those who will 'drop and run' sometimes without saying a proper goodbye to the child for fear of causing them distress. While greater emphasis has been placed on supporting children as they transition into new, different and sometimes multiple learning environments, it is equally necessary to recognise that other family members may also face challenges in adapting and responding to transitions. As we discussed in Chapter 4, attachment plays a key role in supporting a child going through a transition, particularly when there is a change of environment. It is worth noting that parents and carers can also establish strong attachments to staff and the challenges they face when a child moves rooms or leaves the setting altogether will differ.

Degotardi and Pearson (2014) acknowledge that parents can experience a range of emotions when their child transitions from home to formalised care. For many of them, it will be the first time that they are entrusting another adult with the care of their child, which can bring about feelings of nostalgia, distress and guilt (Blatchford et al., 1982; Dalli, 2002).

REFLECTION POINT

Consider how you could support different family members with these different types of transition:

→ Moving to a new room, for example the baby room to toddler room.
→ Moving to a school setting.

(Continued)

(Continued)

→ Experiencing a developmental transition, for example potty training or weaning.
→ Experiencing a personal change of circumstance, for example moving home, a new sibling, bereavement or family breakdown.
→ Multiple transitions occurring at the same time, for example a child moving to a new room in their setting and having a new baby join their family unit.

What would you need to consider in each of these situations? How would you support both children and their families in these circumstances?

As you can see from the reflection above, transitions are not just physical changes to different environments, they can also involve a personal change. It is important to consider the implications personal changes have on families, and even more importantly, to understand when those families may require support from other professionals and services. We shall explore working with other agencies in more detail in Chapter 8.

Several studies have explored the issues and strategies highlighted by parents, practitioners and teachers. One of the most significant barriers to supporting a transition pertains to a lack of communication and information. In situations where there were misunderstandings and misinterpretations, leaders articulated that they would speak to families as quickly as possible, and when things went wrong there were apologies and efforts to make things right. In the majority of cases, these situations were easily resolvable and did not have a detrimental impact on the professional relationship. What happens though when circumstances become more complex? The rest of the chapter shall explore this in further depth.

WORKING IN CHALLENGING CIRCUMSTANCES

In an ideal world children would remain with us until they transition to school, but often this is not the case. Families may move out of the area or personal circumstances may mean that children are withdrawn from settings either officially, for example with the parents giving notice, or in some cases families may just leave. The difficulty with the latter option may have lasting implications for the setting. Families may owe significant amounts of money, with debts having to be written off, or if the child or family require the support of an additional service, the practitioner can no longer make a contribution to their health, care and education plans.

The leaders in our study talked about some of the issues faced when working with family members. While most reported a generally positive experience, a few recalled challenging circumstances that impacted on their practice and professional relationships:

'We spoke about getting him some help and just some more things to support him so he understood, but unfortunately he took it really badly and cancelled her care with me, didn't pay his bill for like two months that he owed and then pulled her out of the school. I went to the school to try and discuss it and support her more, and he pulled out of that school and changed her school, and it turned into quite a horrible sort of messy situation, but it is really hard, because you are just trying to do your job and not all parents understand that, and they do take it really personally that you've just got to keep going and can't take it to heart, and know that as long as you're doing the right thing … some parents are really challenging and difficult'. (Kelly, discussing her previous role working as a nanny for a single-parent family)

'It was very hard. In the end I was taking it personally, because I wasn't getting anywhere, I wasn't achieving … I wasn't getting that kind of trust that I've always managed in the past. It was a real challenge and in the end I just … I'm not going to achieve this because I'm thinking she didn't want me to be here, so I'm talking and working through it. In the end there was one meeting that we had that was kind of "Well I never wanted a nanny and I still don't." I met the dad and said "But that's what I'm battling against and if that's the case of the six months of trying to work this through there's no point in me being here."' (Sarah, discussing difficult relationships with families)

These examples highlight that in some cases there may not be a positive resolution to the challenges that working with families can present. When the practitioners were asked how they dealt with the aftermath of these experiences, they drew attention to the necessity of having the support of their family and friends and being resilient and reflective. Kelly reported how she had used the experience to change her practice, ensuring that she provided a detailed contract and information pack to communicate expectations and procedures to future families. Sarah approached her situation in a different way, by supporting the family with finding an alternative form of provision that better suited their needs. It was evident from the responses participants gave us that the way in which challenges were dealt with were dependent on various individual factors. This ties in with theories pertaining to situational leadership, as devised by Hersey and Blanchard and Fiedler's Contingency Model. Both refer to the context in which leadership can be applied, taking into account a range of variables such as the environment, structure, circumstances of the issue and individual behaviours. Leadership styles may then be adapted to address the situation being presented (Daft, 2011). So what happens when situations escalate and cross professional boundaries?

DEALING WITH AGGRESSION

There will be occasions when situations may escalate to the point where there is a complete relationship breakdown and a potential risk to the practitioner. Parents' and carers' views on discipline, child care, and even the value of play, can lead to discrepancies, which will require the practitioner to intervene and act as a mediator (Wise, 2007). Our interviewees reported that their relationships with parents were generally amicable, and when there was a conflict of interest communication and negotiation were key to resolving difficulties. In some cases these incidents were due to a lack of education or knowledge on issues, such as pedagogical approaches to learning. Regardless of the sector or role worked in, the practitioners and professionals articulated how trust and interpersonal skills addressed areas where there was the potential to be misinterpreted. On rare occasions when communication channels and negotiation were ineffective, some settings reported how parent attitudes and responses became more aggressive and intimidating. In these cases the manager would consider staff safety, and if need be that parent would not be permitted to enter the premises for a specified period of time.

Within the education sector such occurrences are described by Brown and Winterton (2010) as 'parent rage', and can incorporate aggressive behaviours ranging from verbal abuse, intimidation and threats to physical assault. These behaviours are not just confined to the classroom, as the rise in social networking has provided alternative ways for families to potentially harass staff. This can be comprised of posting insulting, offensive and inappropriate comments and making malicious slurs and false allegations (NASUWT, 2015). While these findings are specific to those working in primary and secondary education, this does not mean that parent aggression against early childhood practitioners is non-existent, rather that it is an under-researched area. For those who are at the receiving end of these behaviours, there is a risk of lasting implications for educators' confidence and mental health, leading to stress, anxiety or depression (ATL and ITV regional news, 2014).

In other cases, practitioners and professionals who work closely with one or more families may be on the receiving end of negative behaviour as the direct result of a parent's actions or inactions. This was the case in some of the interviews carried out with nannies and childminders, who reported that they were often held accountable for any difficulties arising at the school or relating to the child or children in their care. One nanny described how miscommunications between the family setting and child's school led to a head teacher accusing her of ruining a child's education.

In these situations it is about the balance of knowing when to be assertive and knowing when to 'leave' the situation, namely removing yourself from the situation, finding some space, and reflecting on how to move forward. Chapter 3 explores in more depth the behaviours and strategies that may be adopted when dealing with aggressive behaviours, and you may wish to refer back to that content and consider how you could apply this in your work with families. The general consensus from our interviews was that the majority of incidents were rectifiable, and communication was key to dealing with misunderstandings or misinterpretations. For leaders, such as nannies and childminders, their close relationships with families placed greater weighting on their ability to be effective communicators, as conflict could lead to job losses or loss of business. There are times where family circumstances can make it more challenging to find an amicable or positive resolution, and we will look at some examples of this in the next section, as we consider more complex issues that families can face.

FAMILIES, ILLNESS, DISABILITIES AND MENTAL HEALTH

According to Meadows (1996), conditions such as depression are likely to impact on a parent's or carer's ability to scaffold children's learning and facilitate their social interaction. As discussed in Chapter 2, children may be placed with foster carers and other family members in situations where a parent or parents are unable to provide an adequate standard of care, often due to illness, disability or addiction (Farmer & Moyers, 2008). In a number of cases a child will remain with their family, with the following examples demonstrating some of the challenges and strategies when practitioners and professionals work directly with these family units:

> 'She will have very good days where she is really happy and really high, really chatty and really good company, and she would then have a few days where ... It was hard because sometimes she wouldn't even get out of bed, as a little boy this is very hard ... From one day to the next his mum was there reading stories and having fun games, and then to the next day not even wanting to see him. So it is hard work, especially for a little boy to understand this and that it's his mummy, and it wasn't until quite late that I understood that she was suffering from bipolar and I think things like that ... I know it's a very private thing but I think when you are work-ing with a unit like that it's important to know, because then I researched it and understood it more, and then I understood more of what she was going through'. (Sarah, discussing the impact of working with a parent diagnosed with bi-polar disorder)

> 'When I first arrived the mother was unable to get out of bed, so knowing that her children were well cared for and sort of receiving consistent care and all that sort of thing was obviously very important to her, it meant that she was able to sort of let go of all those worries at least and concentrate on herself'. (Melissa, discussing her work with a mother who had postnatal depression)

Here, the leaders recognised the challenges parents faced, and through fur-ther discussion they explained the importance of early childhood practitioners researching medical conditions to understand the impact these had on the par-ent and family unit as a whole. Research skills are a crucial component of the reflective cycle, as they provide new information and evidence to inform decision-making processes and actions. In cases where parents had an illness or disability, practitioners would seek alternative means of communication to ensure that they could still offer a high level of support. The relationships with the family were key in addressing changes to personal situations, and having empathy and under-standing was deemed a valuable asset for supporting professionals and families through difficult times. There was also the acknowledgement that for a child attending a setting or receiving care from a nanny or childminder provided stabil-ity and consistency, which was deemed just as crucial in supporting them while the parent or carer was receiving treatment.

FAMILY BREAKDOWNS

It is inevitable that practitioners will be exposed to a diverse range of family set-ups, with an increasing number of families comprised of step-parents and step-children. The practitioners in our study acknowledged that in cases where family situations were having a direct impact on children, they had to maintain a professional stance and address those issues directly with the parents or carers:

> Mercy works as a childminder and became aware of a change in the behaviour of a child in her care. She addressed this concern with the child's mother, who revealed that the family were experiencing a breakdown, which had led to both parents temporarily separating. Mercy addressed the issue by talking to both parents separately, drawing attention to the impact the situation was having on their child. She signposted the family to a relationship counsellor and provided pastoral care by listening to their needs.

In Mercy's case, she recognised a family in crisis and recommended other services that would be suitable for supporting the parents. She revealed that her recommendations led to the parents reconciling some of their differences and coming to an arrangement regarding finances and care of the child. Family difficulties may require the use of other services and professionals and practitioners might wish to have contact numbers and service details available to forward to families in need. The onus is then on the parents to choose whether they seek this support, so unless there is a considerable risk to the child, it is ultimately a parent's responsibility to seek support.

SAFEGUARDING EARLY CHILDHOOD STAFF

One of the key responsibilities that all of us have as early childhood practitioners and professionals is our duty of care to the children using our services, ensuring they are kept safe. Safeguarding is not limited to children and families, as practitioners we must also ensure that we protect ourselves from risk. The term 'keeping safe' differs according to the context it is applied to. For example, nannies and childminders reported that being lone workers required a lot of planning and preparation. This included having contact numbers for families and their wider network, for example other childminders, communicating the times they were expected to leave or arrive at destinations, and also making sure their insurance covered them in emergency situations. Risk assessment was seen as another crucial aspect for those who were self-employed, with many arranging for additional insurance policies to cover children in their care during emergencies.

Several practitioners in group settings highlighted the risks associated with false accusations by parents and children, which was an area of real concern. They reported that they were particularly cautious in their practice and worked on avoiding situations where that practice could be questioned. This was seen to be a serious risk to their profession and perceived to have long-term implications on their future practice. Having policies in place is one way of ensuring that staff and individuals are aware of what to do in circumstances that may impact negatively on their work. It is equally vital that families, visitors and other professionals are fully aware of these policies and have access to them. Keeping records of incidents and accidents is also a means of keeping staff safe, as there is then written evidence to refer to in cases where accusations or allegations have been made. While this may reveal a darker side to working in early childhood, it is something that needs to be at the forefront of practice. With increasingly diverse family units comes an increase in diverse issues and challenges. Therefore the need to have robust policies, procedures and professional boundaries in place is crucial in protecting the needs of both families and practitioners. It is important to recognise that being exposed to conflict and negative relationships can have a detrimental impact on leaders' mental health, particularly if a situation becomes a long drawn-out process. In Chapter 5 we considered the factors that affect staff wellbeing, thus it is worthwhile that we review the content to consider its implications for working with families.

REFLECTION POINT

If you are currently working or planning to work in a setting, which safeguards are in place or what would you expect to be in place to protect you as a professional?

What could you do as a practitioner to ensure that you are protected against the issues raised?

SUMMARY AND CONCLUSIONS

This chapter has explored a number of challenges and considerations when working with diverse family groups and some of the strategies practitioners apply to their work. While working with families brings many rewards, it is equally necessary to understand the implications for practitioners when things do not run smoothly, or when families are affected by a range of factors that challenge their ability to successfully care for their child. In these cases, it may be well beyond the practitioner's remit to fully support the family, hence the next chapter will explore how we can collaborate with other professionals and services, ensuring that families receive the best level of care and support to address individual circumstances and modern family life.

RECOMMENDED FURTHER READING

To explore this topic further, Ward's book is likely to be of interest to you:

Ward, U. (2013) *Working with Parents in the Early Years*, 2nd edn. Exeter: Learning Matters.

8

WORKING WITH OTHER PROFESSIONALS

CHAPTER OBJECTIVES

→ Discuss the various ways in which interprofessional working is experienced.
→ Consider the role of the early childhood leader within a multi-skilled environment.
→ Identify the specialist roles that an early childhood leader may take on.
→ Discuss the ways in which an early childhood leader can work with staff from other professions.

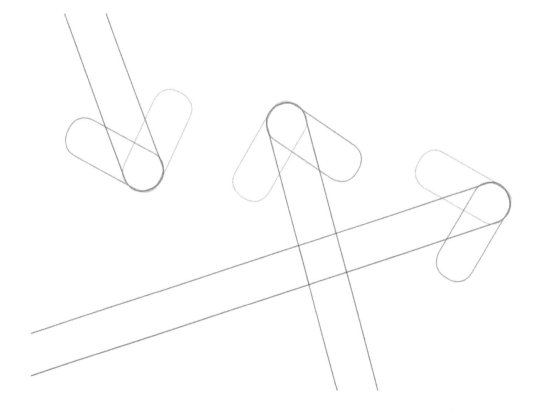

INTRODUCTION

In Chapter 7, we discussed some of the more challenging aspects of practice that arise from working with families, which may be outside of an early childhood leader's professional remit. In this chapter we shall explore how practitioners collaborate with other agencies and professionals across the education, health and social care sectors. There are three sections related to working with other professionals who support and complement the roles and responsibilities of those working in a variety of settings. The first section explores working in a multi-skilled environment, where leaders work in collaboration with a range of services and providers in a specific setting. The second section looks at the specialist roles that early childhood leaders may adopt within their setting, and this leads into the final section on working with other staff in other professional groups.

There are numerous terms used to define the collaboration between early childhood practitioners and professionals from other sectors. These include 'transdisciplinary', 'integrated', 'holistic' and 'multi-agency', which may be used interchangeably (Atkinson et al., 2007). In this chapter we use the term 'interprofessional', which centres on collaboration between two or more parties, with an emphasis on learning with, from, and about each other (CAIPE, 2002). We feel this term supports our ongoing theme of reflection as the emphasis here is on the sharing of skills, knowledge and working together to improve outcomes and reflecting on the impact of interventions (Bridge et al., 2011). On a final note, it is important to understand the relationships between professionals as well as the contexts and constraints in which they work, as roles, responsibilities and practice are prone to changes, and this should be taken into account when collaborating with external agencies (Leadbetter et al., 2007).

WORKING IN A MULTI-SKILLED ENVIRONMENT

The diversity of the early childhood sector means that not all practitioners will be based in private or maintained settings. Alternative environments such as children's wards, hospices, prisons, and even cruise ships, will be comprised of a mix of individuals with different skills and qualifications working collaboratively. Early childhood practitioners may therefore be part of a much wider team, with various leadership structures and hierarchies. Children's centres have been at the very heart of coordinated services, which are derived from consecutive government policies and reports, such as *Meeting the Childcare Challenge* (Scottish Office Education and Industry Department, 1998), *Every Child Matters* (DfES, 2003) and the *Early Years: Foundations for life, health and learning* (Tickell, 2011b). These publications draw attention to the importance of developing effective partnerships between a range of providers, to support the needs of the most vulnerable and disadvantaged families. The development of Sure Start aimed to integrate the delivery of core services, including outreach, healthcare and support for those with special educational needs (Glass, 1999). The term 'multi-agency' has hence been used as a descriptor of this amalgamation of services, but the term suggests that while more than one agency may be supporting a child and family, this may not necessarily be a joint effort (Rawlings & Paliokosta, 2011).

Leadership within children's centres has been supported through the introduction of the National Professional Qualification in Integrated Centre Leadership (NPQICL), a programme aimed at providing children's centre leaders with a professional qualification. Ang (2011) reports that the leadership and coordination element of the children's centre leader's role is integral when working with other agencies. The NPQICL course, in addition to being highly reflective, explored the professional practice of other professions and disciplines, so that leaders were clear on the roles and responsibilities of those whom they would be collaborating with. This training element gave rise to an increased level of understanding, mutual respect, communication and collaboration between the children's centre leaders and other service providers (NCSL, 2008; Tickell, 2011b). Despite the success of the programme, in August 2014 the National College of Teaching and Leadership (NCTL) announced that it had closed, and thereafter made the training sources publicly available for settings and organisations to use as part of alternative professional development and learning (NCTL, 2014).

While children's centres may be one of the most familiar settings in relation to working with other professionals, there are other environments in which early childhood provision acts as an auxiliary component to a wider service. Mother and Baby Units (MBU) located in the prison service provide a high standard of care and education in line with Ofsted standards and regulations. Their aim is to support the needs of mothers and babies up to the age of 18 months, through the use of education, supporting attachments and sharing information with other professionals. These units may be run as crèches, sessional care or full care, depending on the establishment they are based in. For early childhood practitioners, as well as organising and running the nursery facilities, they additionally focus on supporting mothers in forming attachments with their babies and educate them on aspects of care. This role includes liaising with professionals such as the MBU Governor, social workers, disciplinary staff and rehabilitation teams (HM Prison Service, 2008; Holmes et al., 2010). Working in such an environment poses a number of challenges pertaining to risk and the safety of staff, mothers and children. On the one hand, the child and mother are at risk of insecure attachments, and a lack of contact with a wider network of family or community services. On the other hand, the mother may have a history of using substances which affect her ability to care for her child. There may also be specific risks to staff within the MBU, including risk of injury. Additionally, the settings are more isolated compared to other forms of provision (North, 2005). However, mechanisms to promote the wellbeing of mother and baby, and reduce the risk to staff, include specific training for staff and an admissions procedure which the mothers apply through, and gain approval for acceptance into the MBU (Treen, 2011). For practitioners working in these environments, their interprofessional role is particularly vital. Liaison with the MBU Governor, social workers, disciplinary staff and rehabilitation teams is crucial to ensure that the safety and wellbeing of mother and baby are addressed and to enhance the opportunities for positive outcomes.

There are also roles based in healthcare, in which early child practitioners under-take a supportive role, such as working in a neonatal unit under the supervision of a midwife or registered nurse, or as a Health Play Specialist (HPS), formerly known as a Hospital Play Specialist (Williams, 2012). Their job is primarily to lead children, by using play as a therapeutic tool to prepare them for invasive or painful procedures, support rehabilitation, provide a family-centred approach to care, and make a contribution to clinical judgements through observations and documenta-tion (NAHPS, 2012). Although they are not therapists or play leaders, HPSs play a key part in children's recovery and allow them to make choices and understand their options (DH, 2003). They bring expertise in early childhood pedagogy and child development, playing a significant role in relational agency. Furthermore, they act as a voice to uphold a child's right to have a say in relation to their treatment (Nuttall, 2013). These roles may be undertaken in hospitals, hospices, community-based settings and the child's home, and are deemed to be an asset by healthcare professionals (Tanaka, 2010). Working with children with illnesses and life-limiting conditions is a highly emotive experience. In these circumstances Parsons (1991) recommends affective neutrality, in which professionals avoid becoming emo-tionally involved. However, palliative care nurses in a study by Maunder (2008) opposed this approach, and preferred to get to know children and families as a means of assessing their care needs. When working in such emotive environments, the nurses reported that team work was integral, as a means of receiving emotional support from colleagues. In this case again, the team is an interprofessional one.

REFLECTION POINT

When working in an environment with other professionals, how would your team sup-port you or your colleagues in highly stressful and emotive circumstances?

How would you access additional services when meeting the needs of a diverse range of children and families?

These examples of alternative interprofessional working highlight how children and families are at the very heart of provision, regardless of the personal challenges they may be experiencing. As leaders it is important we consider the implications of working within such environments for our professional identity and wellbeing. For example, what support networks are in place when dealing with highly emotive situations? How do interprofessional teams manage in emergency and crisis situa-tions? In Chapter 3 we discussed the ways in which teachers developed emotional resilience by developing strong support networks, and by making sure they focused on their achievements when things had been very emotionally demanding at work (Howard and Johnson, 2004). The importance of making sure staff do not blame themselves when faced with emotionally demanding situations was also empha-sised here, as was the value of learning from experience. The work of Elfer (2012) and Elfer and Dearnley (2007), which we discussed in Chapter 4, is also useful here. Their guidance on how the emotional work of early childhood can be supported through reflection and discussion within the team after a stressful event highlights the need for reflective team work. Reflection through discussion after a challenging event can be a useful way of supporting the emotional wellbeing of staff.

Whatever the multi-skilled environment, it will prove invaluable if you are familiar with the various roles, the areas of expertise those people have, and the sources of support available to you in different circumstances.

DEVELOPING A SPECIALISM

Since the early days of the nursery nurse, practitioners have encompassed numerous roles and responsibilities aimed at supporting the needs of children and their families. In recent years, the development of coordinator roles has paved the way for new leadership responsibilities, in relation to specific aspects of practice or provision. In our interviews with early childhood professionals, there was clear evidence that managers and leaders adopted additional specialist roles, such as the Safeguarding of Children Coordinator (SOCCo), as a means of meeting the statutory requirements set out by the Early Years Foundation Stage (EYFS) and other national and local policies. Another common role was the Special Educational Needs Coordinator (SENCO). All schools are required to have someone appointed to this role, and other early childhood settings are *expected* to have this. All the settings that participated in our research had a named SENCO, and for early childhood leaders in lone worker roles they were primarily responsible for monitoring and reporting any areas of concern to parents, and contacting professionals from their wider networks if they required further advice or support.

To understand a coordinator role, it is necessary to unpack what it entails and what it means for early childhood teams and families. If we look specifically at the SENCO role, that person is responsible for the following:

→ Ensuring all practitioners in the setting understand their responsibilities to children with special educational needs (SEN) and the setting's approach to identifying and meeting SEN.
→ Advising and supporting colleagues.
→ Ensuring parents are closely involved throughout and that their insights inform action taken by the setting.
→ Liaising with professionals or agencies beyond the setting.

(Department for Education, 2015b)

From this specification the role entails much responsibility, and having additional external support is important to ensure the SENCO is able to access the resources, funding and additional support required. Two of our interviewees mentioned that their support came from the Local Authority and Area SENCO, particularly when they were carrying out assessments or needed advice or contact with professionals or services. This level of support is important, as having confidence, expertise, experience and ability is vital for individuals undertaking the role of SENCO. Drifte (2010) states that SENCOs can consider their role to be broad, and carrying this out may make them feel they are not using their specific skills. She warns SENCOs not to feel de-skilled or doubtful about their ability to carry out the role effectively. Rather, she advises them to recognise the 'expertise, experience and abilities' (2010: 24) that they develop within this role. While a newly appointed SENCO is likely to lack confidence, this will be gained quickly through working in the role and with other professionals to guide best practice. However, it is nevertheless important to be mindful of this initial lack of confidence and to avoid over-estimating their skills and abilities. A lack of confidence can deter practitioners from changing their practice and seeking professional learning (Holtom et al., 2015). There are circum- stances in which SENCOs or other early childhood practitioners may be required to coordinate teams of professionals when working with vulnerable families and children with additional needs. One role that can be undertaken by a wide range of professionals across the early childhood workforce is that of Lead Professional, who is responsible for the coordination of the actions identified through the Common Assessment Framework (CAF) (CWDC, 2009a; 2009b).

For early childhood professionals, becoming a Lead Professional can be an over- whelming experience, due to working with a diverse range of professionals. While the majority felt they were capable and brought sufficient skills to the role, others felt they did not receive enough support and aspects of the role were deemed anxiety- provoking (Oliver et al., 2010). This supports our earlier comment by Drifte (2010) that confidence plays a significant role, not just for SENCOs, but also for anyone who has taken on a more specialised role. A key factor that supports the devel- opment of confidence is training, which was highlighted by Siraj-Blatchford and Siraj-Blatchford (2010) as important for those working as Lead Professionals. In Chapter 5 we explored the implications learning and training had on the confidence and skills of leaders undertaking further study. Regardless of whether training or study is long- or short-term, it plays a vital role in supporting leaders with identify- ing their skills, capabilities, and relationships with families and professionals alike.

A further role which may be undertaken in a setting is the Equality Named Coordinator (ENCO). If another member of staff is working in this capacity, they will work alongside the SENCO to support disability equality, in addition to ensuring the equality needs of all children and families in the setting are met (Early Support and Daycare Trust, 2012). For SENCOs, accepting the ENCO as an additional role allows them to oversee all inclusion and equality procedures, but there is a risk that having a dual-role of this nature, combined with other leadership responsibilities, could become an overwhelming task. In Chapter 5 we discussed the implications that excessive paperwork has on the health and wellbeing of early childhood practi- tioners. Atkinson et al. (2002) and Atkinson, Jones and Lamont (2007) recommend setting up support networks and encouraging delegation to other senior staff as a means of placing less pressure on coordinators. In much larger settings or those which have a majority of children with additional needs, there may need to be more than one individual taking responsibility for the aforementioned roles. This could ideally be split, so that one leader is accountable for children aged between birth and 30 months, and the other was responsible for children aged over 30 months.

Specialist roles may also arise from local need or via new initiatives, often with the support of professionals in other sectors. For example, the Early Years Physical Activity and Nutrition (EYPAN) pilot programme was a collaborative project between early childhood practitioners and the National Health Service (NHS) in Cambridgeshire, England. Its aim was to develop a strategy to tackle childhood obesity and provide specialist training and support for practitioners undertaking a new Physical Activity and Nutrition Coordinator (PANCo) role (CEDAR, 2012). In schools, literacy coordinators play an integral role in supporting trainees and newly qualified teachers with raising the standard of language and literacy (Ofsted, 2012). While this role is predominantly aimed at qualified teachers in maintained settings, Ryder's visits to private day nurseries and children's centres uncovered a similar coordinator role that centres on the EYFS Communication, Language and Literacy, in response to an increased focus on phonics and school readiness. These are just some examples of a growing number of roles and positions being developed to ensure that policies are being effectively met, and are in response to an increased focus on providing evidence for Ofsted and being accountable for children's learning and development.

ACTIVITY 8.1

→ Considering the roles and responsibilities above, what skills or expertise would early childhood leaders need to ensure they worked effectively?
→ What do you feel are the challenges when undertaking coordinator roles and how might these be managed?

We hope you have considered the importance of communication in your response for Activity 8.1. Effective communication can lead to better working relationships and stronger outcomes, and can also reduce misunderstandings. You might also have listed other specific skills, such as finding out about policy and processes, and knowing what support is available, for example from the local authority or professional groups. Taking on a new role often requires the development of specific knowledge, for example knowledge of best practice for working in a particular field, and knowledge of policy. Support for these is often found within the professional press and professional organisations, as well as coming from other professionals.

WORKING WITH PEOPLE FROM OTHER PROFESSIONS

Thus far we have explored the professional relationships that can be developed with practitioners and specialists from the health, education and social care sectors. In addition to these, we must not forget that practitioners from the early childhood sector may also count as 'other professionals', particularly when there are significant differences in roles. For example, Melissa discussed how her role as a parent consultant was comprised of running workshops for parents and staff at a local, private day nursery. Her training workshops were a means of supporting other colleagues' professional development, and an opportunity to share her unique experience as a nanny and maternity nurse. Valarie, a private nursery manager, was also involved in training, having worked with a school in Europe to introduce the Reggio Emilia approach to staff. In comparison, Mercy disclosed that in addition to her work as a childminder, she also ran a youth programme to support young people. This was a cause she was passionate about and keen to develop further with the help of a number of contacts within her local community. These findings highlight the multi-faceted nature of working within the early childhood sector, with growing opportunities to use skills and expertise as a means of supporting other professionals and services across the industry.

While we have explored the advantages of working with other professionals and services, there are also limitations and barriers to be mindful of, particularly for managers and leaders who coordinate services. Firstly, there may be a lack of in-depth understanding pertaining to the different agencies worked with and knowledge may also become outdated (Ward, 2011). Secondly, there is a risk that information may be withheld by different agencies: the issue of accountability may become confused if roles and responsibilities are not defined, and risk thresholds can be too high and potentially could impact on professionals being able to carry out preventative work (Home Office, 2014). While these are specific to findings in a report on Multi Agency Safeguarding Hubs (MASH), they are applicable to any form of interprofessional working, such as in the capacity of a Team Around the Family (TAF) or supporting children and families with transitions to schools and other settings.

In response to these challenges, a study by Cartmel et al. (2013) considered a number of aspects that their participants deemed vital to the success of integrated practice within the early childhood sector. For early childhood leaders, the components listed below closely match the interactions and relationships they have in general, but it is worth being mindful here as to how these are transferable when working with professionals with very different levels of training and expertise:

→   Open and honest willingness to accept others' contributions.
→   Sharing and respecting others' professional knowledge.
→   Feeling comfortable with uncertainty.
→   Ensuring each person's experience is made explicit and to be knowledgeable about and comfortable with each person's limitations.
→   Relationship building.
→   Strong leadership skills.

One means of meeting some of the requirements above is through professional development, which was articulated by *Every Child Matters* as a way of building the structures required to ensure professionals across the early childhood workforce could collaborate (DfES, 2003). However, the issue of continuing professional development (CPD) brings its own challenges, as research has identified that costs, funding, difficulty in releasing staff during the day and limited incentives for training have a significant impact on practitioners and leaders accessing training (Condie et al., 2009; Nutbrown, 2012). In turn, this has the potential to support Ward's (2011) previous comment regarding knowledge becoming outdated. It is difficult to provide a solution in these times of austerity, but having strong connections across the sector is one way of keeping up to date with policy developments and changes to roles and practice, and this allows leaders to learn from others.

The ways in which agencies work together are changing, in response to a more holistic approach to support the needs of both children and families. A study by Edwards et al. (2009: 66) identified common concepts used across several Local Authorities, which we feel are applicable to early childhood leaders working in an interprofessional capacity. These include 'focusing on the whole child in the wider context', 'knowing how to know who can help', and 'taking a pedagogic stance at work'. The first concept correlates with several regions around England replacing the CAF assessment with an Early Help Family Assessment (EHFA) form or Family Common Assessment Framework (FCAF). These have been introduced as a means of addressing the wider family problems that are a root cause of difficulties for children. Use of this framework can identify gaps in current support services, as well as taking into account multiple needs which may not be met by current services (Sheffield City Council, 2013; Brighton and Hove Local Safeguarding Children's Board, 2014). In Chapter 7 we drew attention to families who may be experiencing illness, disability and addiction which can have a significant impact on their ability to care for their children. These newer assessment methods are designed to take into account the kind of support those families would need from a wide range of professionals and services. The assessment also links to the second concept by Edwards et al. (2009), in terms of professionals using it as a means of addressing complex problems and identifying the strategies and services needed. The final concept links to professional 'multilingualism', which is defined as communication over professional boundaries and recognising the importance of distributing expertise. Our interviews with Sarah-Jane and Jo highlighted that early childhood leaders would work closely with caseworkers and the Local Authority to support each other's roles. For example, information would be exchanged and other specialists could then visit a setting, observe the child, and liaise with the key person.

Working with children and families in challenging circumstances requires that early childhood practitioners have a strong network with trusted interprofessional colleagues. Building relationships with other professionals takes time, organisation and commitment. When Rose started as a manager at a private day nursery, she identified the benefits that connecting with the local children's centre would bring with regard to her practice and that of her colleagues. Her initial step to learn more about their services, and the way in which health visitors carry out checks on two-year-olds, led to her reflecting on the future needs of the children and families who attended her setting. During her interview for this book, she said:

> 'I wanted to ensure that we were doing the best of what we could do from the setting really, and whether health visitors could come in to us or we could meet with them. The lady was very proactive and came with a couple

of support workers for a visit, and it is informative for her to know about the provision in the area as well. I didn't have any children at the setting that needed one-to-one funding, but I was pre-empting that. It's nice to know what services the children's centre offer. It is about taking a proactive attitude, and if something does arise, I'm not then having to start from scratch. I know who to go to for support, and I know where to direct families too if need be'.

From this example, Rose was proactive in her efforts to connect with another service within her local area and the outcome was positive, with an established relationship between the nursery and children's centre flourishing. Participants in other interviews also made reference to their work with local schools, with teachers visiting the setting to support children transitioning to school. Despite the different locations and roles worked in, a common factor across the interviews was the significance of communication and research, which were seen as an integral step to developing and maintaining partnerships. While initial contact is obviously vital, sustainable relationships arose from our participants keeping in touch and up to date with the other professionals and services they worked with.

SUMMARY AND CONCLUSIONS

This chapter has taken into consideration the diversity of interprofessional working, with a focus on collaborations with other professionals at an internal and external level. The development of coordinator roles has resulted in early childhood professionals being proactive in leading, not only the teams within their setting, but also other service providers and individuals who may be required to support families and children or a specific aspect of provision. There are still many challenges and barriers that affect leaders' ability to formulate effective partnerships, but there are also strategies that can address problem areas. The examples from our interviews have highlighted the importance of planning and timing in taking the first steps to connect with other establishments.

RECOMMENDED FURTHER READING

Some sources which will enable you to explore interprofessional working further include:

Allen, S. (2011) 'Leading practice in a multi-professional context', in M. Whalley and S. Allen (eds), *Leading Practice in Early Years Settings*, 2nd edn. Exeter: Learning Matters. Chapter 8.

Rawlings, A. and Paliokosta, P. (2011) 'Learning for interprofessionalism: pedagogy for all', in L. Trodd and L. Chivers (eds), *Interprofessional Working in Practice: Learning and working together for children and families*. Maidenhead: Open University Press. Chapter 4.

9

IMPROVING LEADING THROUGH REFLECTION

CHAPTER OBJECTIVES

➜ Consider the meaning and value of reflecting on practice.
➜ Discuss opportunities to reflect both alone and with others.
➜ Undertake reflection on practice.
➜ Identify the use of reflection within the role of the leader.
➜ Consider the dangers of reflection.

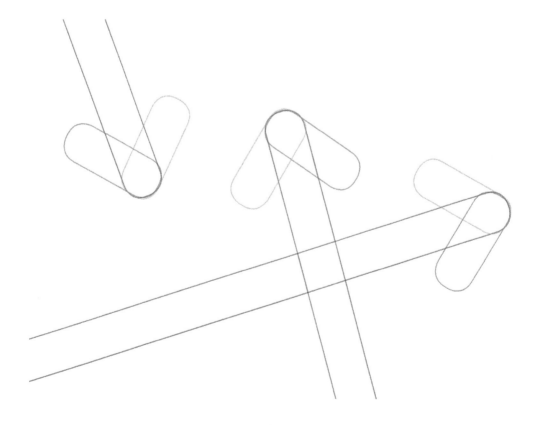

INTRODUCTION

This chapter is about using reflection to enhance your leadership skills. We hope that you will find some of the ideas familiar, but others may well be new to you. If you already use reflection to consider your practice you will know how useful it can be, and how it can lead to changes which will benefit yourself, as well as the children and families and other staff. We see reflection as a vital element of early childhood practice, something both to value and develop. We hope this chapter will not only support you to reflect on your own practice as a leader, but will also help you to support others to develop their skills in reflection.

Being a reflective practitioner means having the ability to think analytically about your own professional practice, to think about what is happening and why it is happening, to consider how things could be done differently, to support best practice. You might already think about what happens at work, but reflection goes further. A leader uses reflection to consider the complexity of issues and their context, and in doing so they turn these thoughts into positive mechanisms to make things better next time round. So from your experiences, both positive and less so, you can gain a better insight into what is happening in your professional practice, and in so doing you can reflect to support improvements in practice. This is different from learning something theoretically, because the world of practice is 'complex, unpredictable and messy' (Finlay, 2008: 3). But by using reflective practice effectively, theoretical knowledge can be drawn from and applied to practice to make improvements in practice.

Towards the end of this chapter, we warn against the negative consequences of reflection. Reflection should be used supportively, to focus on what is going well and how things that are going less well could be improved. We support the use of reflection to celebrate effective practice, but reject using reflection as a tool for instigating change for the sake of change.

WHAT IS REFLECTION?

Reflection is a way of thinking about your practice in order that you can learn from what has happened and either make changes to improve that practice or confirm that it is effective. We have included an entire chapter on reflection here because we consider it to be a crucial way of developing practice, and this includes leadership practice. We all have experiences in our daily working lives, but deliberate effort enables us to learn from these experiences. It is this form of deliberate reflection that we are concentrating on in this chapter. We see reflection as being something that can be carried out alone or with others, formally or informally, and can be part of personal professional development. However, we also believe, like Finlay (2008), that reflection has the potential to be dangerous if it is not used wisely, and therefore we have included some words of caution.

There are a large number of models or theories of reflective practice, and we do make reference to these here. However, we do not want to begin by rehearsing these models as there are already some excellent texts which consider a number of these (for example Ghaye, 2011). We are more interested in getting to grips with reflection as a professional attribute. Reflection in early childhood settings can be a way of thinking about a situation which has occurred, or a way of using experience in planning our next steps. Reflection can also be done 'on the job': typically this means that during the course of the working day, you will make small changes to the way you work to ensure best outcomes.

REFLECTION POINT

To what extent do you see yourself as a reflective practitioner? Can you give examples of your reflective practice?

WHY USE REFLECTION? REFLECTION AS A PROFESSIONAL ATTRIBUTE

There is a good reason why reflective practice has become such a key element of education for early childhood practitioners. Work becomes a source of experiences from which to learn and improve practice. Learning theoretical concepts is important, for example learning about child development or time management, but to become an effective practitioner this theoretical learning needs to be supplemented with the application of that learning to practice. If we take time management as an example, you may have learned about ways to plan, use a diary, and prioritise urgent and important items over your non-urgent and more routine tasks. However, the reality of work can make us challenge our understanding. What do you do, for example, when there are three parents who are all in urgent need of communication but the setting is about to close? Do you see them all at the end of the session? How do you choose between them or prioritise them? Being able to reflect on the real world of work, in relation to theoretical knowledge and understanding, enables us to move from being novices to becoming expert practitioners.

This concept of the value of practice and work-based learning has been advocated for many years across education and care settings (for example Benner, 2001; Hallett, 2013). As a new entrant to an early childhood practitioner role, understanding theoretical concepts such as child development, how children learn, team work and communication is very important. But theoretical concepts only have practical value to children if they can be interpreted and applied in the different contexts of those children and settings. Applying theory comes about through experience in settings and via observation and discussion with more experienced practitioners and reflection on these experiences. In Chapter 2 we considered how reflection ties in with the OPERA system and supports leaders to develop effective learning opportunities for children.

In the example above concerning three families that are all in urgent need of communication, your knowledge of the parents' circumstances (for example, they have another child to collect, they need to get back home so their partner can leave for work, you could ask one of them to see you the following morning) will support you in making rational decisions about these things. And you will learn

by experiencing these everyday real work challenges. As an early childhood practitioner you are in a role which requires you to be professional. Learning to use
reflection to improve practice is part of that professional role.

So what might we want to reflect on? In fact the list is not fixed because work
is not static. Possible items for reflection include: how you manage your time; how
space is managed within a room or within the setting; ways in which you show you
care; how you communicate; how you manage resources; the suitability of different
resources to support each child's development; the ways in which you work with
children, staff and parents; the ways in which the setting works with the multidis-
ciplinary team. You can also reflect on specific incidents which occur in the course
of everyday practice, or specific elements of your role (for example, your role in supporting children's learning). You could take a broad topic to reflect on, for example
ways in which the setting supports a quality environment. Reflection can be specifically used as a tool for your own development, reflecting on your own strengths and
development needs and also on the ways in which you learn best.

ACTIVITY 9.1: CHOOSING WHAT TO REFLECT ON

Re-read the paragraph above and choose one or more areas of your practice or your
role which you want to reflect on. Make a note of these. Two or three topics are
sufficient for now.

   As you read the rest of the chapter, and carry out the activities, keep these topics
in mind to support your reflection.

There are many ways in which reflection can occur. The following sections explore
some of these and ask you to develop your reflection.

REFLECTING ALONE

Reflecting on your own can occur anywhere. For us, reflecting alone tends to occur
more commonly away from work. In these cases that reflection is after the event and
thinking can be free of the other elements of the workplace. For example, on the
journey home you may think about something that happened during that day and
try to make sense of it. Or on a day off you might find yourself having helpful ideas
about how to tackle an issue in practice. In fact one of the benefits of having a break
at work is that your mind can set aside some of the more immediate and pressing
issues so that more time can be spent on reframing problems which have occurred.
In our view, reflection does need some thinking space, some time, and it may also
require a conscious effort to make the time needed to reflect.

   Garvey and Lancaster (2010: 29) suggest that reflective practice can support
many elements of our work: thinking about how we make decisions; how we relate
to others; whether we have gaps in our understanding or knowledge; thinking
about what training we might need; considering how best to deal with difficult

situations. Different authors have recommended a variety of ways of more formally reflecting on practice. These include drawing, using mind maps, using free writing, and writing letters but not sending them (Garvey & Lancaster, 2010). All of these techniques enable us to get our ideas down on paper so that we can see them, and this can then help us to think about these. Hallet (2013) recommends the use of reflective questions, asking yourself the what, how, who, when, where, and why questions to help you understand and get to grips with an issue. The use of reflective journals is also recommended, and as authors, researchers and practitioners ourselves we recommend that you keep a reflective journal, and that you might want to start this with the points you identified in Activity 9.1. For example, keeping a reflective journal, for personal and/or professional reflection, can assist in more formally working through our ideas about an issue. Many people keep very informal reflective journals, others have a more formal structure, such as writing a description of an event, evaluating it, and planning actions to make changes (Hallet, 2013).

ACTIVITY 9.2: DEVELOPING YOUR REFLECTION

Choose just one of the items which you identified in Activity 9.1 and which you think you can reflect on alone. Now choose a technique which you prefer, and make a note of everything that is relevant to your reflection. For example, you might want to draw the different aspects of the issue in your reflective journal, or make a list of the various thoughts you have about the issue, or you may want to write about these, or if it is an issue full of emotion you might want to write a letter (but not send it).

Once you have done this, move on to the next section.

The aim of Activity 9.2 is to elaborate on the detail of the issue you have identified. You may not always want to make a written record of your reflections, but for this activity doing so helps to illustrate the reflective processes you are using. Mackinnon (1993) describes a relatively simple but effective model of reflection. The first step is to identify the initial issue or problem, to 'construct' the problem. This is what you have begun to do in Activity 9.2. The next step described by Mackinnon (1993) is to think about the problem from different angles (see Activity 9.3). For example, you could think about an issue from the point of view of parents, of the child, or a new employee. By doing this you are reframing the problem, seeing it differently. Once you are able to do this, you may be able to see how things could be changed. This is an important step in resolving the initial problem. As Hallet (2013: 25) states, reflection is a step in considering the need to change and 'the purpose of reflective practice is to provide better quality experiences for children and their families'. Hallet (2013: 29) describes reflection as a 'behaviour', and we agree that it is essential to build this behaviour of reflection into practitioners' everyday activity. However, at the level of leadership we would argue that there is also a need to engage intellectually with thinking about our practice. This may include reading about a particular issue in a journal, a book, a guidance document or similar, or it may involve using models or theories of leadership to support reflection.

ACTIVITY 9.3: REFRAMING THE ISSUE

For this activity use your notes from Activity 9.2 where you identified the different elements of the issue from your own point of view as a practitioner and leader of practice. Answer each of these questions about the issue you are reflecting on:

→ How do the family, child, other staff perceive this issue? Do they perceive it in the same way as I do? If not, what are the differences? Here you may have to do some work to discover these viewpoints, for example by talking to those involved.
→ What are the policy or practice guidelines about this issue? These might be national policies or guidelines, or guidelines within your institution, or guidelines from early childhood professional organisations. The policy and practice guidelines may be readily available to you, or you may have to search for these.
→ What research has been done into this issue, and how does this impact on the issue? You may be able to access the research through practitioner journals or professional organisations. Practitioners who are university students will be able to search early childhood journals through the university library. You may also be able to use the local university library through a collaborative arrangement within the local community.

Answering these questions may take some time. This time is worth investing for reflection which aims to support effective practice.

Schön (1996) recommended focusing less on problem solving and more on identifying what the problem is. He used the term 'reflection-in-action' (1996: 19) to think about the activity as it is happening, and to make immediate changes to improve the outcome. Many authors identify a linear or cyclical structured model of reflection, and such models can be very useful for organising your thoughts and moving from thinking to action (for example Dewey, 1933; Schön, 1983; Gibbs, 1988; Johns, 1995; Mezirow, 2000). However, reflective practice is not 'a simple cyclical, linear or static state' but a 'constantly tangled tapestry, an evolving process of weaving theory and practice' (Jones, 2014: 347). We do not work in simple settings but complex ones, and we relate to many different people in the course of our work.

Now that you have made a start on reflecting on an issue from your role or from practice, consider the scenario below which explains the mechanism one practitioner has used to deliberately reflect on her practice. This example was provided by a practitioner who was a participant in the research we carried out for this book. We have not used the practitioner's real name, for reasons of confidentiality.

SCENARIO 9.1: WAYS TO REFLECT

Janette, a key person working in the room for under twos, explained that she reflects on her daily work by using the forms provided by her setting, but that she also reflects on specific issues:

(Continued)

(Continued)

'Here we do development forms, we each do that on our daily practice, if we think we've done something we're really pleased with, we write it down and reflect and that goes upstairs to management, and that is helping me to progress ... because it shows what I am doing well and how I am reflecting on and improving my practice. I do it daily on my day's work. Also if I have set myself a task, a new one, I identify the task, how the children interacted with it, and what I want to do next'.

The development forms were a structured way of reflecting, and a useful mechanism to support the concept of reflection as a professional attribute and develop a culture of reflection in practice. They enabled Janette to get her ideas and notes down on paper, but were also used to support her development as a practitioner. In this case the development form was a simple A4 sheet enabling a practitioner to describe the activity or experience, reflect on the outcome and how things might have been done differently, and then set next steps for practitioner development.

Asked about how she gets her ideas for new activities with the children, Janette stated:

'We have a high quality, table-top activity book and we use that. It has links to the EYFS suited to specific ages and stages, and we are always talking to each other, and bouncing ideas off each other, and it is fairly open downstairs so we can go between rooms to get new ideas'.

In this way, the practitioners were sharing their effective practice with each other. Janette then indicated that there may be information from her reflection on the success of activities that she wanted to pass on to others. There were a number of ways to do this:

'Any information we want to pass on we can put it in the book, about the child, or the nursery, or the room, or an activity, and we have an inspiration board up there. If we see a new activity, or anything we have created, we can put it up on the board'.

These ideas were then discussed at staff meetings so that sharing of effective practice was built into the routine of the setting.

Although the focus of this section has been about reflecting alone, this will frequently include seeking opinions and advice from others. At times, however, our reflection must be initiated with others.

REFLECTING WITH OTHERS

Finding time to reflect alone can be invaluable, but so also is finding time to reflect with others. In Chapter 8 we considered how leaders may work with a range of agencies and professionals to support the more complex needs of children and families. In these circumstances, reflection allows all parties to consider the skills and expertise they have to offer and work coherently to develop effective strategies and interventions. The importance of finding places where all practitioners are able to reflect, including those who have not reflected before on their practice, is something which the overall leader of the setting needs to plan for. Cable and Miller (2011) suggest that the space for reflection must be supportive and allow for development. They link reflection to the notion of both personal and professional learning, but emphasise that it should be linked to action to improve practice.

Reflection with others is part of professional learning (Cable & Miller, 2011; Hallet, 2013). It can be initiated by the practitioner themselves, a mentor or manager, or a colleague. It can also be initiated by something which a child or member of the family will identify. Once the reflection has been initiated, it can include specific observations related to the issue, and seeking out more information, drawing from books, journal articles, experts or other sources of knowledge in the field. Discussion of these observations of practice with colleagues, and drawing on the relevant knowledge, can enable recommendations for change to be made to improve practice. This way of working acknowledges that both vocational and theoretical reflection contribute to new knowledge and understanding of practice.

Elfer (2012) undertook research with nine nursery managers about work discussion. He considers the importance of 'professional reflection', and believes that practitioners 'should have an opportunity to talk through the emotional demands of such work' (2012: 131). This is significant research because it acknowledges the emotional elements in the work of the early childhood practitioner, and recognises the need to build in time to reflect on the emotional work in settings within the staff group as well as other issues. This practice of professional reflection could be planned by the setting manager in a number of ways. For example:

→   Weekly meetings to reflect on an issue.
→   A process of recording ideas about an issue during the course of a week/fortnight/month, and then discussing these at a staff meeting.
→   Professional conversations during the daily schedule between practitioners, including senior staff.

The importance of openness in such reflective discussions is identified by Elfer (2012), although we would argue that this relies implicitly on trust within a team and developing such openness may initially require work to be done on trust. Effective, open, professional discussions will not occur if there is a lack of trust between the various practitioners in a setting. Equally, a lack of trust between practitioners will mean that criticism may be taken personally rather than as an opportunity to reflect and improve practice. The value of work discussions, or professional reflections, lies in the opportunity to deal with the emotion of professional work, as well as in the chance for staff to identify and solve the problems themselves and hence improve practice.

We include below a scenario within a setting which included a number of people. As you read through this account, consider whether such opportunities for group reflection are available in your own setting, either at work or outside of it. For this account consider the following questions. What was the issue? Who identified the issue? How was it explored? Who was involved in the reflection? What mechanisms were used to support the reflection? What was the outcome of the reflection?

SCENARIO 9.2: REFLECTING TOGETHER TO IMPROVE PRACTICE

Here is an account from a practitioner who was one of our participants in the research we undertook for this book:

'I had a child in my room, when he came to nursery he was fine and always happy and a confident learner, but when he got picked up he put on a show and would play up and look sad for his mum and dad. His parents said he was quiet and shy at home, and they were worried. The child would say he was not happy at nursery, the parents were really concerned'.

The practitioner explained that she initially reflected on the situation with the practice leader in the setting, who suggested that this reflection would need to include the other practitioners and the family. The family's perception of their child at the setting was very different from the practitioners' view. A strategy was devised to enable the parents to trust the practitioners' perspective. This was done via a process of videoing the child at the setting and providing these videos to the parents, through frequent communication about what the child had done during the day at the setting and the happy and confident behaviour he had displayed, and by devising an action plan which was jointly followed by the setting and the family. Gradually the family realised that the child had learned that 'if he displayed negative behaviour, he would get the attention of the family'. The action plan enabled a focus on the child's positive behaviour, which then reinforced his positive behaviour. It took several months to change the negative behaviour and confirm to the family that the child was happy in the setting. The practitioner explained the process of detailed formal reflection which supported development within the setting:

'Every week when we do our planning, at the end of the week there is a section which asks us to reflect on all the activities. So we can think about what went well, and what didn't, and what might be the next steps. How could the child best be supported the next week or next fortnight? Also, when we do observations, we write long observations which go to the parents every month, and I will reflect what the child has done, and the parents can write their comments, and you can find out more about what they do at home, and reflect on how you can bring that into the planning too'.

It is very clear from this scenario that the issue was identified jointly between the practitioners in the setting and the family. Reflection was a process which continued until the issue was resolved; it had a positive focus. Exploration of the issue required video observation, careful record keeping, and detailed communication with the family. Time was provided to enable the family to trust the practitioners before an action plan was used to support the child's positive behaviour.

REFLECTING FOR LEADERSHIP

So far in this chapter, we have considered reflection as a component of the practitioner role in relation to all aspects of their work. In this section, we specifically consider the way that reflection is linked to leadership. The ELEYS study (Siraj-Blatchford & Manni, 2007) was an important exploration of existing literature and research about what constitutes effective early childhood education leadership. It considered both patterns of leadership and characteristics of leadership in settings which had been identified as effective. The researchers identified that as changes occur with children, with families, with staff, or within the setting, the role of the leader includes being able to be reflective so that change can be enacted effectively. The strong leaders evident in this study enabled their staff to talk about their work and share their experiences and expertise, including sharing learning from training they had attended. In so doing, there was a recognition that knowledge was not just held by one person, but that every practitioner potentially had knowledge and experience to share and from which others could learn. Encouraging professional conversations, the work discussions (Elfer, 2012) mentioned in the section above, is a key element in leadership. We have already referred to the fact that these work discussions require time and space if they are to be done formally. Part of leadership is to identify the time and space for such discussions to take place. These reflections can be linked to staff development and the identification of development needs. Authors such as Hallet (2013) consider the ways in which vocational progression can occur through reflection. Leaders can plan regular, for example daily, reflective meetings for these professional conversations. We must remember that reflection does not have to be exclusively formal, though encouraging a culture where it is an expectation does require leadership.

Part of the leader role is to model a setting's values and culture. To be able to develop and maintain a culture of learning through reflection, leaders can develop a 'common commitment to reflective, critical practice and professional development' (Siraj-Blatchford and Manni, 2007:16). Effective leaders will go even further, and identify structures within the setting that will enable a 'routine collaborative review' (2007: 15). Such structures will support the effective management of change. Embedding reflective practice in the culture of a setting is linked to enabling change to be seen as a positive part of that setting, rather than something which is imposed, because its community of practitioners are used to working collaboratively and reflecting on practice to improve practice.

To complete this section, here is a scenario from a practice leader in a large setting which is part of a national organisation. This practitioner was a participant in the research we undertook for this book.

SCENARIO 9.3: HEADS OF EARLY YEARS PRACTICE (HOEYP) – LITERACY DEVELOPMENT

In this scenario, an early childhood setting practice leader describes how literacy was first identified for development, and then how changes were made:

'There is a team of Heads of Early Years Practice in this organisation, and we meet once a month to plan more strategic work within the organisation, to make sure the organisation is forward thinking and that we are keeping on top of new ideas, and keeping on top of what is best, and giving the best quality to the children and the parents, and developing good staff. Our ideas are shared as a group, and we reap the rewards when the ideas are put into practice. For example, the reading and writing programme we put together some time back now, came from children's interest and parents' wishes, and us feeling there was a bit of a gap in terms of literacy development and wanting to prepare the children in their transition to school and a more targeted approach, but it is really about them learning to develop a love for literacy rather than just being able to read and write. It is fairly child- led, and based on the children's interest, in terms of the activities on offer around the reading and writing programme. When we first decided to embark on this, we did lots of research about what local schools were doing with reading and writing, and it fits with the Development Matters, the Early Years outcomes, the EYFS, and knowing the development of children at that age and stage, and we started by developing our own flash cards, the team of HOEYPs did this. So we created these flash cards based on the letters and sounds approach, and word banks too to get children to read some simple words, we invested in a wide selection of texts for the children, fiction and non-fiction, and different early childhood and primary education schemes. We have a letter workbook which we do with the children, and the idea is that we give them the activities to do at home too, and it is not about one-to-one reading, it is about the group, ensuring their children have access to the range of materials and making it continuous provision with the home and family. High quality learning opportunities'.

'We introduced this change through training. Anything new, we would have a session after work when the nursery closes, as a group and introduce a new idea. But also in my role I can role model practice within the room, demonstrating practice, leading practice, demonstrating to the team, the way we support the children with this. We are always reflecting on practice, and we put a lot of emphasis on our reflective practice cycle. We make a point at least twice a year of going through our reflective practice cycle, and at that point we will reflect on what has happened over the last few months, so at that point we would reflect on how something new had worked. Reflection happens at both the HOEYP meeting and within the setting, reflection happens here with the team'.

In the scenario above, the heads of early years practice are using their combined experience and the contexts of their various settings to identify and introduce a strategy for engaging children in a love for reading. The joint reflection, consideration of policy, theory and practice, and careful consideration of the training needs to implement the change are evident in this scenario. The scenario also evidences the leaders' recognition of their responsibility in role-modelling best practice and taking time with staff in their setting to reflect on the success of the changes implemented.

REFLEXIVITY

The chapter thus far has looked at reflection and reflective practice. This section considers another element of reflection, reflexivity. Cable and Miller (2011: 154) identify the notion of reflexivity as 'the ability to understand one's own impact on a situation or event and one's contribution to meaning making' as taking a route to being more professional. Being reflexive is therefore more than reflecting. It is difficult to be reflexive when you are learning something new, but when you are an experienced practitioner you will be in a position to think critically about the effect you have at work, on parents, on children, on members of staff. It takes considerable confidence and self-awareness to be able to be reflexive and turn this reflexivity into improved practice. As a leader of others' professional development you will need to support the workforce to talk about their own understandings of their role, what, why and how they do things, and how this affects others. Supporting others to develop critical reflection takes experience and confidence. Colmer (2009) identified the value of a network of early years colleagues to support leaders to be critically reflective and enable them to develop their own leadership skills and abilities.

The various sections within this chapter have emphasised the importance of reflection to improve practice. The next section considers some examples. As you read through these think about how you can make use of them for your own development as a reflective practitioner.

SOME SCENARIOS FOR REFLECTION ON PROFESSIONAL PRACTICE

The scenarios below relate to the professional attributes of early childhood practitioners, drawn from material covered in previous chapters. Even if you are an experienced practitioner, we would hope that you will gain some insight from these reflections.

ACTIVITY 9.4: REFLECTION ON ASSERTIVENESS

Each day, for one week, think back and make a note of any occasions where assertive action was required. This might be occasions when you consider you have not acted assertively, or ones where you did act assertively. We recommend that you have at least three situations to think about. For each of the situations, make a note of the behaviour and actions you displayed. For example, you may have been submissive, non-assertive, aggressive, or avoided facing a situation.

For each of the occasions which you have identified, think about how an assertive person might have responded. If you did act assertively, consider why this was effective and whether different behaviour could have influenced the situation. Use the examples and discussion below and refer back to Chapter 3 to help you.

In Chapter 3 we considered ways to become assertive. This activity makes use of your own experiences to frame ways to act assertively. Here is an example of a situation. Your manager is strong willed and you find her intimidating. You like your job but dare not suggest how to make changes for fear of her shouting at you. Today was a lovely day, albeit cold and wet underfoot, and you wanted to take the children into the garden. Your manager said 'I know it is lovely out there but no way am I going to be responsible for Johnny getting muddy, his mother will be furious'. You decided not to take the children into the garden.

Think about how you can move from the situation described above to a situation where you would be able to take the children into the garden in a similar situation.

This is likely to include several considerations:

→   You might think of reasons to agree with the manager, for example: she is likely to be angry if Johnny gets muddy; the mother does get furious; you do not want to be held responsible. On the other hand, you know about the value of outdoor play, and that getting muddy is not necessarily a bad thing.
→   You might consider the fact that you never stand up to this manager because you find her so intimidating.
→   When you have thought through the situation, you can then consider small steps which could assist you in achieving the goal of outdoor play for children in a similar circumstance. But these need not be directly related to the circumstance. For example, you might identify an opportunity not to be intimidated by the manager, but to stand up to her, and this could be over a small thing to start with. You might want to discuss with the parents about suitable outdoor clothing. You might want to identify the value of outdoor play and create a display about this. Think about how you could deal with each of the components that you identify, and practise this in front of a mirror, or in front of a friend.

How did you get on with your reflections on your own assertive behaviour at work from Activity 9.4? If required, revisit Chapter 3 to support your assertive behaviour. Remember to focus on your successes, and what worked well. Extending these to other aspects of your work will give you a greater sense of empowerment in your role.

The following activity asks you to reflect on your resilience at work.

ACTIVITY 9.5: REFLECTION ON RESILIENCE

In Chapter 3 we discussed the Australian study by Howard and Johnson (2004). These researchers found that resilient teachers had strong support mechanisms that included family and friends as well as support within the work setting. These strong support mechanisms supported teachers' resilience by giving them a sense of agency, a belief that they could make a difference at work. In this activity, reflect on the following possible support mechanisms. Identify the extent to which each of these is available to you, and the extent to which you might make greater use of them.

→   I have supportive family/friends outside of work.
→   I have opportunities to discuss issues with colleagues at work.
→   I trust other staff, they are capable and professional.
→   I am trusted by others as capable and professional.
→   The leaders in the setting are supportive.

Use your responses to these items to consider whether you need to plan changes to support your own resilience, or to be supportive of others' resilience. Note that undertaking these activities is not meant to be a quick fix.

Your responses to Activity 9.5 may demonstrate that you have a strong support network which effectively enables your resilience at work. You may, however, have identified some aspects of that support which you could enhance, for example learning to trust and be trusted in your professional role, or creating opportunities to discuss issues with colleagues. There may be some elements which you are not able to change. Working to improve those support mechanisms that can be changed rather than focusing on matters outside your immediate control will give you a greater sense of ownership and influence within your professional role. Remember, reflection is intended to make you feel empowered to be more effective. It is not intended to focus on the unchangeable aspects of your role. Keep in mind the positive attributes you possess.

The activities above are meant to help you think about your own situation, and if necessary to plan changes to improve that situation. Ongoing reflection is important in helping you maintain your professional awareness of your skills and attributes, and taking steps to support your further development. As a leader, some of the issues on which you may wish to focus reflection could include:

→   the way in which you respond to criticism;
→   the way you communicate with other staff, with children, with families, and with the multiprofessional team;
→   how you make use of theoretical concepts to improve your leadership practice;
→   reflecting on your espoused values and beliefs and how these are manifest in your practice;
→   the way in which you set realistic goals for improving practice;
→   how you role model reflective practice;
→   how you celebrate effective practice.

You will no doubt want to reflect on many things, but the list above should give you some ideas to support effective reflection which has the potential to enhance practice across the setting.

THE HIDDEN DANGERS OF REFLECTIVE PRACTICE

While we fully support the use of effective reflective practice to enable practitioners to think about how things are done, and to make recommendations for changes in how these are done, we are also aware that reflection can be dangerous. It can make practitioners feel incompetent, unskilled and disempowered. It can also be difficult to do effectively. Superficial 'checklist'-type reflection may result from a requirement to reflect when work is busy and staff are stressed: as Finlay (2008: 10) indicates, 'bland, mechanical, routinized and unthinking ways of doing reflective practice' can occur if lip service is paid to reflection. So while we have made reference to a number of reflective practice models in this chapter, we do not want you to rigidly follow a pattern of reflection just for the sake of doing so. We would encourage you to reflect when something prompts you to. This prompt may be a discussion with a parent or child, an idea you have when planning or organising an activity, an incident which occurs in the setting, something you read about a topic which is relevant to your own setting,

So what are the specific dangers of reflective practice? Finlay (2008) identifies four areas of concern:

→ Ethical.
→ Professional.
→ Pedagogic.
→ Conceptual.

For example, she notes that 'reflection can have a profound emotional impact' (2008: 11) and could therefore cause harm to the individual practitioner who is reflecting on their own practice. This may be at the level of currently feeling secure in ways of working, but as a result of reflection feeling that this security is going to be disrupted and those ways of working will become very different. There is also the danger that reflection becomes so focused on improvement there is no recognition of what is working well, either for the individual or for the setting as a whole. Some work experiences are challenging, and reflecting on these can prove emotionally demanding, and may not be supported within a work context. We would therefore advocate considering that work context, and identifying points for reflection which have the potential for positive outcomes within it. Reflection may not be the most useful tool to address big issues within a setting: these may need to be explored using other strategies, such as critical incident analysis, theoretical reasoning, or an exploration and redefinition of workplace values.

Thinking here about the negative aspects of reflection, we are still advocating the use of reflective practice, but we want to see it used wisely. A new practitioner with little theoretical knowledge of child development or of how children learn may find it very challenging to reflect on practice. However, if reflective practice is tied in with professional development for that practitioner they can support their knowledge and understanding through this reflection. Effective mentoring (see Chapter 5) can be a very useful way of helping practitioners to reflect in ways which will be of benefit rather than harmful. A mentor needs to be able to identify the stage a practitioner has reached, whether novice, experienced or expert, and support reflection that is appropriate to this. In such a way that practitioner's work experiences can be supported through directed reflection into greater knowledge and understanding of practice. Mentors also need to support practitioners in understanding that reflection is a useful tool, but should be used wisely, when it can be helpful, and not as a matter of routine. So just as important as being keen to reflect on practice is our willingness to identify when reflection may not be useful because there is a lack of insight into issues. For example, if as practitioners we reflect alone about an issue which affects our entire team, then we may miss colleagues' perceptions and interpretations of that issue. Therefore, we would advocate thinking about which issues can be reflected on alone, and which ones may need reflection by the team, and which issues may not be suited to reflection at all.

Being able to use reflective practice effectively assumes a context within which a practitioner has a voice, where there is the opportunity to suggest changes to practice, whether these are changes to routines, to policies, to the structure or resources, or other changes. A very useful way in which team reflection can be employed is by sharing after a professional development event, and discussing the application of the learning to the specific setting. Phair and Davis (2015) noted that practitioners who attended development events were often not able to make use of a development within their setting. An opportunity, for example at a staff meeting, needs to be identified to share what was learned and look at any available resources. A team will then have an opportunity to consider the value of such training in their setting, and in this way the development activity will have an effect on the whole team and be more likely to have an effect on the setting also.

SUMMARY AND CONCLUSIONS

Reflective practice is a key element of professional work for the early childhood leader. The purpose of reflection for the early childhood practitioner is to ensure the best possible outcomes for children and families, and in so doing to support the development of professional expertise in practitioners and across the setting. Actively and deliberately reflecting on aspects of practice and professional role can support practitioners to celebrate effective practice and develop areas of practice to make them more effective. Reflective practice may be something which is carried out alone by the practitioner to consider their own ways of working, to celebrate what went well, and to identify the need for training or for change or further action. Reflection can also be carried out with others across the setting and this is important as a mechanism to identify and celebrate effective practice as well as to identify ways in which training, changes in practice, or different uses of resources may enhance practice. Within this chapter, we have stressed the importance of positive reflection. It is a process which requires practitioners to be open-minded, to take responsibility, and to be wholehearted (Hallet, 2013) in their desire to provide the optimal experience to support children and families.

RECOMMENDED FURTHER READING

Hallet, E. (2013) *The Reflective Early Years Practitioner*. London: SAGE.
This book is based on doctoral research, a case study of a foundation degree in early childhood. It is a useful text to support the process of reflection for early childhood practitioners.

REFERENCES

4Children (2013) *Removal of LA's Early Years Quality Role Raises Alarm*. Available at www.4children.org.uk/Files/2815bb82-b722-4f65-97d7-a1880088281a/Out-Of-School-Newsletter-March-2013.pdf (last accessed 11 June 2016).

4Children (2014) *Sure Start Children's Centres Census 2014: A national overview of Sure Start Children's Centres in 2014*. Exeter: 4Children.

Adams, J.S. (1965) 'Inequality in social exchange', in L. Berkowitz (ed.), *Advances in Experimental Psychology*. New York: Academic. pp. 267–99.

Ainsworth, M.D.S., Blehar, M.C., Waters, E. and Wall, S. (1978) *Patterns of Attachment: A psychological study of the strange situation*. Hillsdale, NJ: Erlbaum.

Allen, S. (2011) 'Leading practice in a multi-professional context', in M. Whalley and S. Allen (eds), *Leading Practice in Early Years Settings*, 2nd edn. Exeter: Learning Matters. pp. 115–30.

Allen, S. and Whalley M.E. (2010) *Supporting Pedagogy and Practice in Early Years Settings*. Exeter: Learning Matters.

Ang, L. (2011) 'Leading and managing in the Early Years: a study of the impact of a NCSL Programme on Children's Centre leaders' perceptions of leadership and practice', *Educational Management Administration and Leadership*, 40(3): 289–304.

Ang, L. (2014) 'Introduction: the curriculum in diverse settings: defining curriculum', in L. Ang (ed.), *The Early Years Curriculum: The UK context and beyond*. Abingdon: Routledge. pp. 1–11.

Anning, A. and Edwards, A. (2006) *Promoting Children's Learning from Birth to Five: Developing the new Early Years professional*, 2nd edn. Maidenhead: Open University Press.

Association of Teachers and Lecturers (ATL) (2014) *Pressures on Teachers Causing Rise in Mental Health Issues – ATL*. London: ATL. Available at www.atl.org.uk/Images/11%20 for%2014%20Apr%202014%20-%20annual%20conf%20mental%20health%20 issues.pdf (last accessed 11 June 2016).

Association of Teachers and Lecturers (ATL) and ITV regional news (2014) *Half of education staff have faced aggression from students in the last year*. Press release, 1 September 2014. Available at www.atl.org.uk/Images/Sept%201,%202014%20-%20ATL%20beha viour%20survey%202014%20FINAL.pdf (last accessed 6 April 2015).

Atkin, J., Bastiani, J. and Goode, J. (1988) *Listening to Parents: An approach to the improvement of home-school relations*. Beckenham: Croom Helm.

Atkinson, M., Jones, M. and Lamont, E. (2007) *Multi-Agency Working and its Implications for Practice: A review of the literature*. Reading: CfBT.

Atkinson, M., Wilkin, A., Stott, A., Doherty, P. and Kinder, K. (2002) *Multi-Agency Working: A detailed study* (LGA Research Report 26). Slough: NFER.

Aubrey, C. (2011) *Leading and Managing in the Early Years*, 2nd edn. London: SAGE.

Aubrey, C., Godfrey, R. and Harris, A. (2012) 'How do they manage? An investigation of early childhood leadership', *Educational Management, Administration and Leadership*, 41 (1): 5–29.

Babcock, L. and Laschever, S. (2003) *Women Don't Ask: Negotiation and the gender divide*. Princeton, NJ: Princeton University Press.

Barr, J. and Dowding, L. (2015) *Leadership in Healthcarer*, 3rd edn London: SAGE.

Belsky, J. (1999) 'International and contextual determinants of attachment security', in J. Cassidy and P.R. Shaver (eds), *Handbook of Attachment: Theory, Research and Clinical Applications*. New York: Guildford. pp. 249–64.

Benner, P. (2001) *From Novice to Expert: Excellence and power in clinical nursing practice* (Health Commemorative edition). Upper Saddle River, NJ: Prentice-Hall.

Bennett, J. and Palaiologou, I. (2016) 'Personal, social and emotional development', in I. Palaiologou (ed.), *The Early Years Foundation Stage: Theory and practice*, 3rd edn. London: SAGE, pp. 345–365.

Bennett, N., Wise, C., Woods, P.A. and Harvey, J.A. (2003) *Distributed Leadership: A review of the literature*. National College for School Leadership, Open Research Online. Available at http://oro.open.ac.uk/8534/1/bennett-distributed-leadership-full.pdf (last accessed 30 November 2015).

Bennis W. (2009) *On Becoming a Leader*. New York: Basic Books.

Biringen, Z. (2000) 'Emotional availability: conceptualisation and research findings', *American Journal of Orthopsychiatry*, 70: 104–14.

Blatchford, P., Battle, S. and Mays, J. (1982) *The First Transition: Home to pre-school*. Windsor: NFER.

Boag-Munroe, G. (2014) '"Parents as partners": the new politics of parenting', in J. Moyles, J. Payler and J. Georgeson (eds), *Early Years Foundations: Critical Issues*, 2nd edn. Maidenhead: Open University Press. Ch. 14.

Boag-Munroe, G. and Evangelou, M. (2012) 'From hard to reach to how to reach: a systematic review of the literature on hard-to-reach families', *Research Papers in Education*, 27(2): 209–39.

Bond, M. (1987) *Managing Care Pack 18: Being Assertive, Reader*. London: Distance Learning Centre, London South Bank Polytechnic.

Bowlby, J. (1958) 'The nature of the child's tie to his mother', *International Journal of Psychoanalysis*, 39: 350–71.

Bowlby, R. (2007) 'Babies and toddlers in non-parental daycare can avoid stress and anxiety if they develop a lasting secondary attachment bond with one carer who is consistently accessible to them', *Attachment and Human Development*, 9 (4): 307–19.

Bridge, D.R., Davidson, R.A., Soule Odegard, P., Maki, I.V. and Tomkowiak, J. (2011) 'Interprofessional collaboration: three best practice models of interprofessional education', *Medical Education Online*, 16 (10). Available at www.ncbi.nlm.nih.gov/pmc/articles/PMC3081249/ (last accessed 11 June 2016).

Brighton and Hove Local Safeguarding Children's Board (2014) *Children's Services Threshold Document: A guide to early help and safeguarding services*, Brighton and Hove City Council. Available at www.brighton-hove.gov.uk/sites/brighton-hove.gov.uk/files/BHCC%20Children%27s%20Services%20Threshold%20Document%202014%20rev%2022%20Oct.pdf (last accessed 11 June 2016).

Brind, R., McGinigal, S., Lewis, J., Ghezelayagh, S., Ransom, H., Robson, J., Street, C. and Renton, Z. (2014) *Childcare and Early Years Providers Survey 2013*. Available at: www.gov.uk/government/uploads/system/uploads/attachment_data/file/355075/SFR 33_2014_Main_report.pdf (last accessed 11 June 2016).

British Educational Research Association (BERA) (2011) *Ethical Guidelines for Educational Research*. London: BERA. Available at www.bera.ac.uk/researchers-resources/resources-for-researchers (last accessed 12 October 2015).

Brodie, K. (2013) *Observation, Assessment and Planning in the Early Years: Bringing it all together*. Maidenhead: Open University Press.

Brooker, L., Rogers, S., Ellis, D., Hallet, E. and Roberts-Holmes, G. (2010) *Practitioners' Experiences of the Early Years Foundation Stage.* London: Department for Education.

Brown, J. and Winterton, M. (2010) *Insight 1: Violence in UK Schools: What is really happening?* Macclesfield: BERA.

Bruce, T., Louis, S. and McCall, G. (2015) *Observing Young Children.* London: SAGE.

Burnes, B. (2004) 'Kurt Lewin and the Planned Approach to Change: a re-appraisal', *Journal of Management Studies*, 41: 977–1002.

Burns, J.M. (1978) *Leadership.* New York: Harper & Row.

Cable, C. and Miller, L. (2011) 'A new professionalism', in L. Miller, L. and C. Cable (eds), *Professionalization, Leadership and Management in the Early Years.* London: SAGE.

CACHE (2016) NCFE CACHE Level 3 Diploma for the Early Years Workforce (Early Years Educator) Available at: http:// www.cache.org.uk/Qualifications/EYE/Pages/CACHE-Level-3-Diploma-for-the-Early-Years-Workforce-(Early-Years-Educator)-(QCF)-.aspx (last accessed 11 June 2016).

CAIPE (2002) *Defining IPE: Interprofessional education.* Available at http://caipe.org.uk/resources/defining-ipe/ (last accessed 11 June 2016).

Campbell, C. (2011) *How to Involve Hard-to-Reach Parents: Encouraging meaningful parental involvement with schools.* Nottingham: National College for School Leadership.

Care Council for Wales (2012) *Work Experience in Social Care and Early Years: A guide.* Cardiff: Care Council for Wales.

Carlyle, T. (1869) *On Heroes, Hero-Worship, and the Heroic in History.* London: Chapman and Hall.

Carr, M. (2001) *Assessment in Early Childhood Settings: Learning stories.* London: SAGE.

Carrington, B. and Skelton, C. (2003) 'Re-thinking "role models": equal opportunities in teacher recruitment in England and Wales', *Journal of Education Policy*, 18 (3): 253–65.

Cartmel, J., Macfarlane, K. and Nolan, A. (2013) 'Looking to the future: producing trans-disciplinary professionals for leadership in early childhood settings', *Early Years,* 33 (4): 398–412.

Central Advisory Council for Education (CACE) (1967) *Children and their Primary Schools. Volume 1: Report (The Plowden Report).* London: HMSO.

Centre for Diet and Activity Research (CEDAR) (2012) *Evaluation: Early Years Physical Activity and Nutrition (EYPAN).* Available at www.cedar.iph.cam.ac.uk/research/directory/eypan/ (last accessed 11 June 2016).

Children's Workforce Development Council (CWDC) (2006) *A Head Start for All: Early Years Professional Status candidate information.* Leeds: CWDC.

Children's Workforce Development Council (CWDC) (2009a) *The Team Around the Child and the Lead Professional: A guide for managers.* Leeds: CWDC.

Children's Workforce Development Council (CWDC) (2009b) *The Team Around the Child and the Lead Professional: A guide for practitioners.* Leeds: CWDC.

Children's Workforce Development Council (CWDC) (2010) *The Common Core of Skills and Knowledge: At the heart of what you do.* Leeds: CWDC.

Children's Workforce Development Council (CWDC) (2011) *New Leaders in Early Years Pilot.* Available at http://webarchive.nationalarchives.gov.uk/20120119192332/http://cwdcouncil.org.uk/early-years/graduate-leaders-in-early-years/new-leaders-explained (last accessed 11 June 2016).

Chu, M. (2012) 'Observe, reflect and apply: ways to successfully mentor early childhood educators', *Dimensions of Early Childhood*, 40 (3): 20–8. Available at http://southernearlychildhood.org/upload/pdf/Dimensions_Vol40_3_Chu.pdf

Clark, A., McQuail, S. and Moss, P. (2003) *Exploring the Field of Listening to and Consulting with Young Children*. London: Department for Education and Skills.

Clifford-Poston, A. (2002) 'Stress in childcare: screaming point', *Nursery World*. London: MA Education.

Cohen, B. and Fraser, N. (1991) *Childcare in a Modern Welfare System: Towards a new national policy*. London: Institute for Public Policy Research.

Coleyshaw, L., Whitmarsh, J., Jopling, M. and Hadfield M. (2012) *Listening to Children's Perspectives: Improving the quality of provision in early years settings: Part of the longitudinal study of Early Years professional status*. London: Department for Education.

Colmer, K. (2009) 'Leading a learning organisation: Australian early years centres as learning networks', *European Early Childhood Education Research Journal*, 16 (1): 107–15.

Condie, R., Seagraves, L., Fee, J. and Henry, J. (2009) *Continuing Professional Development of Early Years Managers and Practitioners Working with Children under 3 Years of Age*. Technical Report, Faculty of Education, University of Strathclyde. Available at http://strathprints.strath.ac.uk/26618/1/strathprints026618.pdf (last accessed 11 June 2016).

Cortis, N., Katz, L. and Patulny, R. (2009) *Engaging Hard-to-Reach Families and Children: Stronger Families and Communities Strategy 2004-2009*. Canberra, Australia: Australian Government, Department of Families, Housing, Community Services and Indigenous Affairs.

Curtis, A. (1998) *A Curriculum for the Pre-School Child: Learning to learn*, 2nd edn. London: Routledge.

Daft, R. (2011) *Leadership*. Boston, MA: South-Western Cengage Learning.

Dalli, C. (2002) 'From home to childcare centre: challenges for mothers, teachers and children', in H. Fabian and A.W. Dunlop (eds), *Transitions in the Early Years: Debating continuity and progression for children in early education*. London: RoutledgeFalmer. pp. 38–51.

David, T., Goouch, K., Powell, S. and Abbott, L. (2003) *Birth to Three Matters: A review of the literature*. London: Department of Education and Skills.

Davis, G. (2012) 'A documentary analysis of the use of leadership and change theory in changing practice in early years settings', *Early Years, an International Journal of Research and Development*, 32 (3): 266–76.

Davis, G. and Capes, P. (2013) *Early Years Professional Status Impact Study, Final Report: Achieving outcomes in Essex*. Report for Essex County Council, Anglia Ruskin University. Available at http://hdl.handle.net/10540/295428 (last accessed 20 September 2015).

Davis, G. and Ryder, G. (2015) *Exploring Leadership in Early Childhood Practice: Summary of original research*. Available at http://hdl.handle.net/10540/592966 (last accessed 11 June 2016).

Deforges, C. and Abouchaar (2003) *The Impact of Parental Involvement, Parental Support and Family Education on Pupil Achievement and Adjustment: A Literature Review*. Annesley: Department For Children, Schools and Families Publications.

Degotardi, S. and Pearson, E. (2014) *The Relationship Worlds of Infants and Toddlers: Multiple perspectives from Early Years theory and practice*. Maidenhead: Open University Press.

Denham, S.A. (1986) 'Social cognition, prosocial behaviour, and emotion in preschoolers: contextual validation', *Child Development*, 57 (1): 194–201.

Department for Children, Schools and Families (DCSF) (2007) *The Early Years Foundation Stage: Effective Practice: Parents as partners*. Annesley: Department For Children, Schools and Families Publications.

Department for Children, Schools and Families (DCSF) (2008a) *Early Years Consultants' Handbook*. Annesley: Department For Children, Schools and Families Publications.

Department for Children, Schools and Families (DCSF) (2008b) *The Impact of Parental Involvement on Children's Education.* Annesley: Department for Children, Schools and Families Publications.

Department for Children, Schools and Families (DCSF) (2008c) *Statutory Framework for the Early Years Foundation Stage.* Annesley: Department For Children, Schools and Families Publications.

Department for Children, Schools and Families (DCSF) (2010) *Challenging Practice to Further Improve Learning, Playing and Interacting in the Early Years Foundation Stage.* Annesley: Department For Children, Schools and Families Publications.

Department for Education (DfE) (2012) *Statutory Framework for the Early Years Foundation Stage: Setting the standards for learning, development and care for children from birth to five.* London: Department for Education.

Department for Education (DfE) (2013) *More Great Childcare: Raising quality and giving parents more choice.* London: Department for Education. Available at www.gov.uk/government/uploads/system/uploads/attachment_data/file/219660/More_20Great_20Childcare_20v2.pdf (last accessed 11 June 2016).

Department for Education (DfE) (2014a) *Early Education and Childcare: Statutory guidance for local authorities.* Available at https://www.gov.uk/government/publications/early-education-and-childcare-2 (last accessed 11 June 2016).

Department for Education (DfE) (2014b) *Statutory Framework for the Early Years Foundation Stage.* London: Department for Education. Available at www.gov.uk/government/publications/early-years-foundation-stage-framework—2

Department for Education (DfE) (2015a) *Become an Early Years Teacher.* London: Department for Education. Available at: https://getintoteaching.education.gov.uk/explore-my-options/become-an-early-years-teacher (last accessed 11 June 2016).

Department for Education (DfE) (2015b) *Special Educational Needs and Disability Code of Practice: 0 to 25 years: Statutory guidance for organisations which work with and support children and young people who have special educational needs or disabilities.* Available at www.gov.uk/government/uploads/system/uploads/attachment_data/file/398815/SEND_Code_of_Practice_January_2015.pdf (last accessed 11 June 2016).

Department for Education and Skills (DfES) (2002) *Work Experience: A guide for employers.* Annesley: DfES.

Department for Education and Skills (DfES) (2003) *Every Child Matters.* London: HMSO.

Department for Education and Skills (DfES) (2007) *Every Parent Matters.* London: Department for Education and Skills.

Department of Health (DH) (2003) *Getting the Right Start: National service framework for children: Standard for hospital services.* London: DH.

Dewey, J. (1933) *How We Think: A restatement of the relation of reflective thinking to the educative process* (revised edn). Boston, MA: D.C. Heath.

Dilts, R. (2003) *From Coach to Awakener.* Available at http://theperformancesolution.com/wp-content/uploads/2009/12/From-Coach-to-Awakener.pdf (last accessed 11 June 2016).

Docherty, P., Stott, A. and Kinder, K. (2004) *Delivering Services to Hard to Reach Families in On Track Areas: Definition, consultation and needs assessment.* London: Home Office.

Drifte, C. (2010) *The Manual for the Early Years SENCO,* 2nd edn. London: SAGE.

Eagly, A.H. and Carli, L.L. (2007) *Through the Labyrinth: The truth about how women become leaders.* Boston, MA: Harvard Business School Press.

Early Education (2012) *Development Matters.* London: Early Education. Available at https://early-education.org.uk/development-matters-early-years-foundation-stage-eyfs-download (last accessed 11 June 2016).

Early Support and Daycare Trust (2012) *Information About the People You May Meet.* Available at www.ncb.org.uk/media/875176/earlysupportinformationpeopleyoumaymeet final.pdf (last accessed 11 June 2016).

Education and Training Inspectorate (2014) *An Evaluation of the Role of the Early Years Specialist.* Bangor: Department of Education. Available at www.etini.gov.uk/index/ surveys-evaluations/surveys-evaluations-pre-school-centre-and-nursery-school/surveys-evaluations-pre-school-2014/an-evaluation-of-the-role-of-the-early-years-specialist.pdf (last accessed 23 December 2015).

Edwards, A., Daniels, H., Gallagher, T., Leadbetter, J. and Warmington, P. (2009) *Improving Inter-professional Collaborations: Multi-agency working for children's wellbeing.* Abingdon: Routledge.

Einarsen, S., Aasland, M.S. and Skogstad, A. (2007) 'Destructive leadership behaviour: a definition and conceptual model', *The Leadership Quarterly*, 18: 207–16.

Eisenberg, N., Guthrie, I.K., Murphy, B.C., Shepard, S.A., Cumberland, A. and Carlo, G. (1999) 'Consistency and development of prosocial dispositions: a longitudinal study', *Child Development*, 70 (6): 1360–72.

Elementary Teachers' Federation of Ontario (ETFO) (2011) *Playing is Learning.* Ontario, Canada: ETFO. Available at http://earlylearningcentral.ca/?page_id=1192 (last accessed 11 June 2016).

Elfer, P. (2012) 'Emotion in nursery work: work discussion as a model of critical professional reflection', *Early Years: An international research journal*, 32 (2): 129–41. http://dx.doi. org/10.1080/09575146.2012.697877.

Elfer, P. and Dearnley, K. (2007) 'Nurseries and emotional well-being: evaluating an emotionally containing model of professional development', *Early Years: An International Research Journal*, 27 (3): 267–79. http://dx.doi.org/10.1080/09575140701594418.

Elfer, P., Goldschmeid, E. and Selleck, D. (2003) *Key Persons in the Early Years: Building relationships for quality provision.* London: David Fulton.

Elfer, P., Goldschmeid, E. and Selleck, D. (2012) *Key Persons in the Early Years: Building relationships for quality provision in early years settings and primary schools*, 2nd edn. London: Routledge.

Emerson, E., Hatton, C., Robertson, J., Baines, S., Christie, A. and Glover, G. (2013) *Improving Health and Lives: Learning Disabilities Observatory: People with learning disabilities in England 2012.* London: Public Health England.

Evans, M. (2008) 'EYFS Key Person Training', *Nursery World*, 14 October.

Farmer, E. and Moyers, S. (2008) *Kinship Care: Fostering effective family and friends placements.* London: Jessica Kingsley.

Finlay, L. (2008) *Reflecting on 'Reflective Practice'*, PBPL paper 52. Maidenhead: Open University Press. Available at www.open.ac.uk/opencetl/files/opencetl/file/ecms/web-content/Finlay-(2008)-Reflecting-on-reflective-practice-PBPL-paper-52.pdf (last accessed 7 April 2015).

Frame, L., Orfirer, K. and Ivins, B. (2004) 'Creating threads of continuity: helping infants and toddlers through transitions in foster care', *The Source*, 13 (2): 1–22. Available at http://aia.berkeley.edu/media/pdf/source_vol13_no2.pdf (last accessed 11 June 2016).

Fukada, S., Fukada, H. and Hicks, J. (2001) 'Structure of leadership among preschool children', *Journal of Genetic Psychology*, 155(4): 389–95.

Gabriel, P. and Liimatainen, M.R. (2000) *Mental Health in the Workplace: Introduction executive summaries.* Geneva, Switzerland: International Labour Office.

Garris Christian, L. (2006) 'Applying family systems theory to early childhood practice', *Young Children*, 61 (1): 12–20. Available at www.naeyc.org/files/yc/file/200601/Christian BTJ.pdf (last accessed 11 June 2016).

Garvey, D. and Lancaster A. (2010) *Leadership for Quality in Early Years and Playwork*. London: NCB.

Gaunt, C. and Morton, K. (2013) 'Removal of LA's early years quality role raises alarm', *Nursery World*, 8 February.

Ghaye, T. (2011) *Teaching and Learning through Reflective Practice*, 2nd edn. London: Routledge.

Gibbs, G. (1988) *Learning by Doing: A guide to teaching and learning methods*. Oxford: Oxford Polytechnic FEU.

Glass, N. (1999) 'Sure Start: the development of an early intervention programme for young children in the United Kingdom', *Children and Society*, 13: 257–64.

Goddard, C. and Temperley, J. (2011) *Transforming Early Years: Different, better, lower cost services for children and their families*, GoddardPayne and Temperley Research. Available at www.innovationunit.org/sites/default/files/Transforming%20Early%20Years%20–%20 Learning%20Partner%20Final%20Report.pdf (last accessed 23 December 2015).

Goldschmied, E. and Jackson, S. (2004) *People under Three: Young children in day care*, 2nd edn. London: Routledge.

Goleman, D. (1996) *Emotional Intelligence*. London: Bloomsbury.

Goouch, K. and Powell, S. (2013) *The Baby Room: Principles, policy and practice*. Maidenhead: Open University Press.

Government Equalities Office (2011) *Equality Act 2010: What do I need to know? A quick start guide on the ban on questions about health and disability during recruitment*. Manchester: Government Equality Office.

Gray, P. (1999) *Mental Health in the Workplace: Tackling the effects of stress*. London: Mental Health Foundation.

Green, L. (1968) *Parents and Teachers: Partners or rivals?* London: Allen and Unwin.

Hadfield, M., Jopling, M., Needham, M., Waller, T., Coleyshaw, L., Emira, M. and Royle, K. (2012) *Longitudinal Study of Early Years Professional Status: An exploration of progress, leadership and impact: Final report*. London: Department for Education. Available at www.gov.uk/government/uploads/system/uploads/attachment_data/file/183418/DfE-RR239c_report.pdf (last accessed 20 Seotember 2015).

Hallet, E. (2013) *The Reflective Early Years Practitioner*. London: SAGE.

Harris, A. and Goodall, J. (2007) *Engaging Parents in Raising Achievement: Do parents know they matter?* London: DCFS.

Heikka, J. and Waniganayake, M. (2011) 'Pedagogical leadership from a distributed perspective within the context of early childhood education', *International Journal of Leadership in Education*, 14 (4): 499–512.

Heikka, J., Waniganayake, M. and Hujala, E. (2012) 'Contextualising distributed leadership within early childhood education: current understandings, research evidence and future challenges', *Educational Management, Administration and Leadership*, 41 (1): 30–44. Available at http://ecadmin.wdfiles.com/local—files/leadership-adminis tration/Distributed%20Leadership%20within%20EC.pdf (last accessed 30 November 2015).

Hewett, V.M. (2001) 'Examining the Reggio Emilia approach to early childhood education', *Early Childhood Education Journal*, 29 (2): 95–100.

Hillman, S. and Smith, G. (1981) 'Development of leadership capacities in children', *The Elementary School Journal*, 82 (1): 58–65.

HM Prison Service (2008) *Prison Service Order: The management of mother and baby units*, 4th edn. Available at www.birthcompanions.org.uk/media/Public/Resources/ Extpublications/PSO_4801_management_of_mother_and_baby_units_4th_edition. pdf (last accessed 11 June 2016).

Holmes, R., Jones, L., McClure, M. and Browne, K. (2010) *HM Prison Service Styal Mother and Baby Unit: An appreciative inquiry.* Manchester: Education and Social Research Institute, Manchester Metropolitan University.

Holtom, D., Bowen, R. and Lloyd-Jones, S. (2015) *An Assessment of Special Educational Needs (SEN) Workforce Development Requirements: Final report.* Cardiff: Additional Learning Needs Branch, Welsh Government.

Home Office (2014) *Multi Agency Working and Information Sharing Project: Final report.* London: Home Office. Available at www.gov.uk/government/uploads/system/uploads/attachment_data/file/338875/MASH.pdf (last accessed 11 June 2016).

Howard, S. and Johnson, B. (2004) 'Resilient teachers: resisting stress and burnout', *Social Psychology of Education*, 7 (4): 399–420.

Hughes, M., Wikeley, F. and Nash, T. (1994) *Parents and their Children's Schools.* Cambridge, MA: Blackwell.

Hunt, J., Waterhouse, S. and Lutman, E. (2008) *Keeping Them in the Family: Outcomes for children placed in kinship care through care proceedings.* London: British Association for Fostering and Adopting (BAAF).

Irvine, C. (2012) *Volunteer Now's Response to the Consultation the 'Towards a ChildCare Strategy'.* Belfast: Volunteer Now.

Jackson, S.E., Joshi, A. and Erhardt, N.L. (2003) 'Recent research on team and organizational diversity: SWOT analysis and implications', *Journal of Management*, 29 (6): 801–30.

James, A. and Prout, A. (1996) 'Strategies and structures: towards a new perspective on children's experiences of family life', in J. Brannen and M. O'Brien (eds), *Children in Families: Research and Policy*. Washington, DC: Routledge Falmer. pp. 41–52.

Johns, C. (1995) 'Framing learning through reflection within Carper's fundamental ways of knowing in nursing', *Journal of Advanced Nursing*, 22 (2): 226–34.

Jones, C. (2014) 'Reflective practice', in T. Waller and G. Davis (eds), *An Introduction to Early Childhood*, 3rd edn. London: SAGE. pp. 346–63.

Jones, C. and Pound, L. (2008) *Leadership and Management in the Early Years.* Maidenhead: Open University Press.

Kahn, T. (n.d.) 'Recruiting volunteers', *Teach Nursery*. Available at www.teachearlyyears.com/images/uploads/article/recruiting-volunteers.pdf (last accessed 11 June 2016).

Kanyal, M. and Gibbs, J. (2014) 'Participation: Why and how?, in M. Kanyal (ed.), *Children's Rights 0–8: Promoting participation in education and care*. Abingdon: Routledge. pp. 45–62.

Kelley-Laine, K. (1998) 'Parents as partners in schooling: the current state of affairs', *Childhood Education* 74 (6). Available at Anglia Ruskin University Library website http://libweb.anglia.ac.uk (last accessed 16 April 2015).

Kernan, M. (2012) *Parental Involvement in Early Learning: A review of research, policy and good practice.* The Hague: Bernard van Leer Foundation.

Knowles, A. (2016) 'Working in partnership with parents', in I. Palaiologou (ed.), *The Early Years Foundation Stage: Theory and practice*, 3rd edn. London: SAGE. pp. 251–264.

Kotter, J. (1996) *Leading Change.* Boston, MA: Harvard Business School Press.

Langston, A. and Abbott, L. (2005) 'Quality matters', in L. Abbott and A. Langston (eds), *Birth to Three Matters: Supporting the Framework of Effective Practice.* Maidenhead: Open University Press. pp. 68–78.

Leadbetter, J., Daniels, H., Edwards, A., Martin, D., Middleton, D., Popova, A., Warmington, P., Apostolov, A. and Brown, S. (2007) 'Professional learning within multi-agency children's services: researching into practice', *Educational Research*, 49 (1): 83–98.

Lee, S.Y., Recchia, S.L. and Shin, M.S. (2005) '"Not the same kind of leaders": four young children's unique ways of influencing other', *Journal of Research in Childhood Education*, 20 (2): 132–48.

Lloyd, E. and Hallet, E. (2010) 'Professionalising the early childhood workforce in England: work in progress or a missed opportunity?', *Contemporary Issues In Early Childhood*, 11 (1): 75–88.

Locke, E.A. (1968) 'Toward a theory of task motivation and incentives', *Organizational Behavior and Human Performance*, 3 (2): 157.

Lord, P., Southcott, C. and Sharp, C. (2011) *Targeting Children's Centre Services on the Most Needy Families* (LGA Research Report). Slough: NFER.

Lyford Jones, H. (2010) *Putting Children at the Centre: A practical guide to children's participation.* London: Save the Children UK.

Mackinnon, A.M. (1993) 'Detecting reflection-in-action among pre-service elementary science teachers', in E. Whitelegg, J. Thomas and S. Tresman (eds), *Challenges and Opportunities for Science Education.* London: Paul Chapman. pp. 44–60.

Male, T. (2016) 'Leadership', in I. Palaiologou (ed.), *The Early Years Foundation Stage: Theory and practice,* 3rd edn. London: SAGE. pp. 312–328.

Maslow, A.H. (1943) 'A theory of human motivation', *Psychological Review*, 50: 370–96.

Maunder, E.Z. (2008) 'Emotion management in children's palliative care nursing', *Indian Journal of Palliative Care*, 14 (1): 45–50 [e-journal]. Available at http://libweb.anglia.ac.uk (last accessed 11 June 2016).

McConkey, R. (1985) *Working with Parents: A practical guide for teachers and therapists.* London: Croom Helm.

McElwain, N.L. and Booth-Laforce, C. (2006) 'Maternal sensitivity to infant distress and nondistress as predictors of infant-mother attachment security', *Journal of Family Psychology*, 20 (2): 247–55.

McGillivray, G. (2008) 'Nannies, nursery nurses and early years professionals: constructions of professional identity in the early years workforce in England', *European Early Childhood Education Research Journal*, 16 (2): 242–54.

Meadows, S. (1996) *Parenting Behaviour and Children's Cognitive Development.* Hove: Psychology Press.

Mezirow, J. (2000) 'Learning to think like an adult: core concepts of transformation theory', in J. Mezirow (ed.), *Learning as Transformation.* San Francisco, CA: Jossey-Bass. pp. 3–34.

Mohammed, R. (2014) 'The challenges of implementing early years curriculum: a practitioner's perspective', in L. Ang (ed.), *The Early Years Curriculum: The UK context and beyond.* Abingdon: Routledge. pp. 32–53.

Morgan, G. (2006) *Images of Organization.* London: SAGE.

Moylett, H. and Djemli, P. (2004) 'Practitioners matter', in L. Abbott and A. Langston (eds), *Birth to Three Matters: Supporting the Framework of Effective Practice.* Maidenhead: Open University Press. pp. 56–67.

Murphy, S.E. (2011) 'Providing a foundation for leadership development', in S.E. Murphy and R.J. Reichard (eds), *Early Development and Leadership: Building the next generation of leaders.* New York: Taylor and Francis. pp. 3–38.

NAHPS (2012) *Health Play Specialist Career Information.* Available at http://nahps.org.uk/index.php?page=careers-information (last accessed 11 June 2016).

NASUWT (2015) *Huge Rise in Teachers being Abused on Social Media,* press release, 2 April. Available at www.nasuwt.org.uk/Whatsnew/NASUWTNews/PressReleases/NASUWT_013930 (last accessed 11 June 2016).

National College for School Leadership (NCSL) (2008) *Realising Leadership: Children's centre leaders in action: The impact of the National Professional Qualification in Integrated Centre Leadership (NPQICL) on children's centre leaders and their centre.* Nottingham: NCSL.

National College for Teaching and Leadership (NCTL) (2014) *The National Professional Qualification in Integrated Centre Leadership (NPQICL)* [online] Available at: https://www.nationalcollege.org.uk/?q=node/612 (last accessed 11 June 2016).

National Institute for Health and Care Excellence (NICE) (2015) *Workplace Health: Management practices.* London: NICE. Available at www.nice.org.uk/guidance/ng13/resources/work place-health-management-practices-1837269751237 (last accessed 11 June 2016).

National Mental Health Development Unit (NMHDU) (2010) *Factfile 6: Stigma and discrimination in mental health.* London: NMHDU.

NDNA (2015) *Case Study: Early Years Teacher working with more than one setting.* Huddersfield: NDNA.

Noddings, N. (2003) *Caring: A feminine approach to ethics and moral education,* 2nd edn. Berkeley, CA: University of California Press.

North, J. (2005) *Getting It Right: Services for pregnant women, new mothers and babies in prison.* London: Maternity Alliance.

Northouse, P. (2015) *Leadership: Theory and practice,* 7th edn. London: SAGE.

Nutbrown, C. (2012) *Foundations for Quality: The independent review of early education and childcare qualifications: Final report.* London: Department for Education. Available at www.gov.uk/government/publications/nutbrown-review-foundations-for-quality (last accessed 11 June 2016).

Nuttall , J. (2013) 'Inter-professional work with young children in hospital: the role of "relational agency"', *Early Years,* 33 (4): 413–25.

Office for Disability Issues and DWP (2014) *Disability Prevalence Estimates 2011/12.* Available at www.gov.uk/government/uploads/system/uploads/attachment_data/file/321594/disability-prevalence.pdf (last accessed 11 June 2016).

Ofsted (2012) *From Training to Teaching Early Language and Literacy: The effectiveness of training to teach language and literacy in primary schools.* Manchester: Ofsted. Available at www.gov.uk/government/uploads/system/uploads/attachment_data/file/413204/From_training_to_teaching_early_language_and_literacy.pdf (last accessed 11 June 2016).

Oliver, C., Mooney, A. and Statham, J. (2010) *Integrated Working: A review of the evidence.* Leeds: CWDC.

Osborn, A.F. and Milbank, J.E. (1987) *The Effects of Early Education: A report from the Child Health and Education Study.* Oxford: Clarendon.

Padilla, A., Hogan, R. and Kaiser, R.B. (2007) 'The toxic triangle: destructive leaders, susceptible followers and conducive environments', *The Leadership Quarterly,* 18: 176–94.

Page, J. and Elfer, P. (2013) 'The emotional complexity of attachment interactions in nursery', *European Early Childhood Education Research Journal,* 21 (4): 553–67. http://dx.doi.org/10.1080/1350293X.2013.766032.

Palaiologou, I. (2012) *Child Observation for the Early Years,* 2nd edn. Exeter: Learning Matters.

Palaiologou, I. (2016) 'Effective transitions', in I. Palaiologou (ed.), *The Early Years Foundation Stage: Theory and practice,* 3rd edn. London: SAGE. pp. 213–234.

Parsons, T. (1991) *The Social System.* London: Routledge.

Penn, H. (2011) *Quality in Early Childhood Services: An international perspective.* Maidenhead: Open University Press.

Phair, H. and Davis, G. (2015) 'Early childhood settings and funded two-year-old children: experiences from four settings in England', *Early Child Development and Care*. Available at www.tandfonline.com/doi/full/10.1080/03004430.2014.1003553 (last accessed 11 June 2016).

Pileri, A. (2010) 'Inter-actions: families, children and professionals at the nursery in multicultural contexts: actions-research between Paris and Bologna', in E. Catarsi and J.P. Pourtois (eds), *«Education familiale et services pour l'enfance »* AIFREF 2010, Firenze University Press. pp. 232–237.

Piper, A.M., D'Angelo, S.D. and Hollan, J.D. (2013) 'Going digital: understanding paper and photo documentation practices in early childhood', in CSCW (Computer-Supported Cooperative Work and Social Computing), *16th ACM Conference on Computer Supported Cooperative Work and Social Computing*. San Antonio, Texas, United States, 23–27 February. ACM: New York.

Rah, Y. (2013) 'Leadership stretched over school and community for refugee newcomers', *Journal of Cases in Educational Leadership*, 16 (3): 62–76.

Rallings, J. (2014) *What Are Children's Centres For?* Ilford: Barnardo's.

Rawlings, A. and Paliokosta, P. (2011) 'Learning for interprofessionalism: pedagogy for all', in L. Trodd and L. Chivers (eds), *Interprofessional Working in Practice: Learning and working together for children and families*. Maidenhead: Open University Press. pp. 53–68

Robins, V. and Silcock, P. (2001) 'The invisible professionals: English school nursery nurses talk about their jobs', *European Early Childhood Education Research Journal*, 9 (1): 23–40.

Rodd, J. (2013) *Leadership in Early Childhood: The pathway to professionalism*, 4th edn. Maidenhead: Open University Press.

Rolfe, H., Metcalf, H., Anderson, T. and Meadows, P. (2003) *Recruitment and Retention of Childcare, Early Years and Play Workers: Research study*. Annesley: DfES.

Rose, J. and Rogers, S. (2012) *The Role of the Adult in Early Years Settings*. Maidenhead: Open University Press.

Rowland, V. and Birkett, K. (1992) *Personal Effectiveness for Teachers*. Hemel Hempstead: Simon and Schuster Education.

Royston, S. and Rodrigues, L. (2013) *Breaking Barriers: How to help children's centres reach disadvantaged families*. London: Children's Society.

Scharf, M. and Mayseless, O. (2009) 'Socioemotional characteristics of elementary school children identified as exhibiting social leadership qualities', *Journal of Genetic Psychology*, 170 (1): 73–94.

Scheer, S.D. and Safrit, R.D. (2001) 'Nurturing future leadership skills in five to eight year-old children through self-awareness activities', *Journal for Leadership Studies*, 8(2): 105–11.

Schön, D.A. (1983) *The Reflective Practitioner: How professionals think in action*. New York: Basic Books.

Schön, D.A. (1996) *Educating the Reflective Practitioner: Towards a new design for teaching and learning in the professions*. San Francisco, CA: Jossey-Bass.

Scottish Office Education and Industry Department (1998) *Meeting the Childcare Challenge: A childcare strategy for Scotland* (Cm. 3958). Edinburgh: HMSO.

Scrivens, C. (2002) 'Constructions of leadership: does gender make a difference? Perspectives from an English speaking country', in V. Nivala and E. Hujala (eds), *Leadership in Early Childhood Education: Cross cultural perspectives*. Proceedings of OULU Forum, University of Oulu, Oulu, Finland. pp. 25–32. Available at http://herkules.oulu.fi/isbn9514268539/isbn9514268539.pdf (last accessed 12. October 2015).

Sharp, C., Lord, P., Handscom, G., Macleod, S., Southcott, C., George, N. and Jeffs, J. (2012) *Highly Effective Leadership in Children's Centres*. Nottingham: National College for School Leadership.

Sheffield City Council (2013) *Family Common Assessment Framework (FCAF): Information for workers.* Sheffield: Sheffield City Council.

Shier, H. (2001) 'Pathways to participation: openings, opportunities and obligations. A new model for enhancing children's participation in decision-making in line with Article 12.1 of the United Nations Convention on the Rights of the Child', *Children and Society,* 15: 107–17.

Siraj-Blatchford, I. and Manni, L. (2007) *Effective Leadership in the Early Years Sector.* London: Institute of Education.

Siraj-Blatchford, I. and Siraj-Blatchford, J. (2010) *Improving Development Outcomes for Children through Effective Practice in Integrating Early Years Services.* London: Centre for Excellence and Outcomes in Children and Young People's Services (C4EO).

Smidt, S. (2005) *Observing, Assessing and Planning for Children in the Early Years.* Abingdon: Routledge.

Smidt, S. (2009) *Planning for the Early Years Foundation Stage.* Abingdon: Routledge.

Smilansky, S. (1968) *The Effects of Sociodramatic Play of Disadvantaged Preschool Children.* London: Wiley.

Steiner Waldorf Schools Fellowship (2013) *EYFS Exemptions and Modifications Granted to Steiner: Schools and settings.* Stourbridge: SWSF. Available at www.steinerwaldorf.org/eyfs-exemptions-good-news-for-our-early-years-settings/ (last accessed 11 June 2016).

Sterling Honig, A. (2010) *Little Kids, Big Worries: Stress-busting tips for early childhood classrooms.* Baltimore, MD: Paul H. Brookes.

Sylva, K., Goff, J., Eisenstadt, N., Smith, T., Hall, J., Evangelou, M., Smith, G. and Sammons, P. (2015) *Organisation, Services and Reach of Children's Centres: Evaluation of children's centres in England (ECCE, Strand 3). Research report.* London: Department for Education.

Sylva, K., Melhuish, E., Sammons, P., Siraj-Blatchford, I. and Taggart, B. (2012) *Effective Pre-school and Primary Education 3–11 Project.* London: Department for Education and Skills/Institute of Education.

Tanaka, K. (2010) 'A need for play specialists in Japanese children's wards: play therapy in UK hospitals is well established but in Japan the speciality is still developing, explain Kyoko Tanaka and colleagues', *Paediatric Nursing,* 22 (6): 31–2.

Tickell, C. (2011a) *The Early Years Foundation Stage Review: Report on the evidence.* Available at www.gov.uk/government/uploads/system/uploads/attachment_data/file/184839/DFE-00178-2011.pdf (last accessed 11 June 2016).

Tickell, C. (2011b) *The Early Years: Foundations for life, health and learning: An independent report on the Early Years Foundation Stage to Her Majesty's Government.* Available at www.gov.uk/government/uploads/system/uploads/attachment_data/file/180919/DFE-00177-2011.pdf (last accessed 11 June 2016).

Tizard, J., Moss, P. and Perry, J. (1976) *All Our Children: Pre-school services in a changing society.* London: Temple Smith.

Treen, B. (2011) *Mother and Baby Units.* London: Ministry of Justice.

Touhill, L. (2012) *Inquiry-based learning.* Early Childhood Australia. Available at www.earlychildhoodaustralia.org.au/nqsplp/wp-content/uploads/2012/10/NQS_PLP_E-Newsletter_No45.pdf (last accessed 11 June 2016).

Vincent, C. (1996) *Parents and Teachers: Power and participation.* London: Falmer.

Volunteer Now (2012) *As Good As They Give: Providing volunteers with the management they deserve: Workbook Three Managing and Motivating Volunteers.* Belfast: Volunteer Now.

Ward, U. (2011) 'Mentoring interprofessionally: a concept of practice for peer mentoring in children's centres', in L. Trodd and L. Chivers (eds), *Interprofessional Working in*

Practice: Learning and working together for children and families. Maidenhead: Open University Press. pp. 69–82.

Ward, U. (2013) *Working with Parents in the Early Years,* 2nd edn. Exeter: Learning Matters.

Westat of Rockville Maryland (1998) *Effective Practices of Foster Grandparents in Headstart Centers: Benefits for children, classroom and centers.* Rockville, MD: The Office of Evaluation.

Whalley, M. (2011a) *Leading Practice in Early Years Settings,* 2nd edn. Exeter: Learning Matters.

Whalley, M.E. (2011b) 'Leading and managing in the early years', in L. Miller and C. Cable (eds), *Professionalization, Leadership and Management in the Early Years.* London: SAGE. pp. 13–28.

Williams, C. (2012) *A Background Report on Nurse Staffing in Children's and Young People's Health Care.* London: Royal College of Nursing.

Winter, P. (2010) *Neuroscience and Early Childhood Development: Summary of selected literature and key messages for parenting.* Ministerial Council for Education, Early Childhood Development and Youth Affairs. Available at http://scseec.edu.au/site/Default Site/filesystem/documents/Reports%20and%20publications/Publications/Early%20 childhood%20education/Engaging%20Families%20in%20the%20ECD%20Story-Neuroscience%20and%20ECD.pdf (last accessed 11 June 2016).

Wise, S. (2007) *Building Relationships between Parents and Carers in Early Childhood: AFRC Briefing No.5,* Australian Institute of Family Studies.

Wolfendale, S. (1992) *Empowering Parents and Teachers: Working for children.* London: Cassell.

Woodhouse, J. (2015) *The Voluntary Sector and the Big Society,* Briefing Paper Number 5883. London: House of Commons Library.

INDEX